SURVIVING

CW00524688

About the Author

Diana Mather is a partner in Public Image, a company specializing in helping people to be themselves in front of a camera or microphone. She has extensive media experience, having been an actress, programme presenter and newsreader. These days her time is divided between co-presenting the Executive Business Channel for BBC Select, running media and presentation training courses and writing.

SURVIVING THE MEDIA

*How to appear successfully on TV,
radio or in the press*

DIANA MATHER

Thorsons
An Imprint of HarperCollins*Publishers*

Thorsons
An Imprint of HarperCollins*Publishers*
77-85 Fulham Palace Road,
Hammersmith, London W6 8JB
1160 Battery Street,
San Francisco, California 94111–1213

Published by Thorsons 1995

1 3 5 7 9 10 8 6 4 2

© Diana Mather 1995

Diana Mather asserts the moral right to
be identified as the author of this work

A catalogue record for this book
is available from the British Library

ISBN 0 7225 3010 2

Printed in Great Britain by
HarperCollinsManufacturing Glasgow

All rights reserved. No part of this publication may be
reproduced, stored in a retrieval system, or transmitted,
in any form or by any means, electronic, mechanical,
photocopying, storage or otherwise, without the prior
permission of the publishers.

CONTENTS

ACKNOWLEDGEMENTS

The research for this book has been fascinating, and I sincerely thank all the people I have talked to for squeezing me into their very busy schedules and finding time to tell me about the way they handle a story, produce a programme or write an article. They include: Susie Aplen (Planet 24), Paul Anthony (photographer), Charles Barnett (Clerk of the Course, Aintree Racecourse), Michael Barratt (broadcaster), Mike Becker (ITV director), Lesley Bond (make-up artist), Edward Brady (Public Affairs Manager, ICI Chemicals & Polymers), Cary Cooper (Professor of Organisational Psychology, Manchester School of Management, UMIST), John Chester (BBC cameraman), Joanna Coles (journalist and broadcaster), Delia Corrie (partner in Public Image), Edwina Curry (MP), Ed Doolan (presenter, Radio WM), John Dunn (presenter, BBC Radio 2), Nancy Evans (director of Re-solve), Christopher Fildes (financial columnist, *The Daily Telegraph* and *The Spectator*), Jo Fletcher (BBC production assistant), Peter Godwin (reporter, *Panorama* and *Assignment*), Felicity Goody (BBC North reporter and presenter), Roy Greenslade (journalist and editor), John Gurnett (producer, *Jimmy Young* programme), Judyth Halpin (partner, First Impressions), Philip Harding (editor of news programmes, Radio 5 Live), Peter Harrison (writer and broadcaster), Philip Hayton (BBC presenter and newscaster), Eamon Holmes (presenter, *GMTV*), John Humphries (presenter, *Today*), Sir Bernard Ingham (journalist and ex-press secretary to Margaret Thatcher), Charles Kennedy (MP), Robert Kilroy-Silk (presenter, *Kilroy*), Neil Kinnock (MP), Christine Livingstone (BBC studio technician), Sue McGregor (presenter, *Today*), Gabrielle Morris (freelance journalist), Derek Monk (EBC producer and director), James Naughtie (presenter, *Today*), David Parry-Jones (editor, *Chester Chronicle*), Jeremy Paxman (presenter, *Newsnight*), Ann Reevell (senior producer, BBC radio features), Adam Roscoe (Hill and Knowlton PR), Chris Rush (Media & Public Relations Officer, Salford City Council), Roy Saatchi (head of local programmes, BBC North), Sir Bob Scott (chairman of Manchester's Commonwealth Games Bid Committee), Tony Scull (Yorkshire Television and EBC producer and director), David Shepherd (artist and conservationist), Geoff Simpson (Public Affairs Manager, CWS), Sue Stapeley (head of press and Parliamentary affairs at the Law Society), Jonathan Taylor (BBC radio producer), Adrian Tomlin (sound recordist), Christopher Walmsley (television and radio producer and presenter), George Westropp (National Director of Communications, Touche Ross), Sarah Wetherall (partner in Public Image), Tony Wetherall (sound recordist), Jo Wheeler (presenter, Radio Lincolnshire), Peter Wheeler (broadcaster and partner in Public Image), Terry Wheeler (BBC and EBC producer and director), Amanda Winkworth (television director), Nicholas Witchell (BBC newscaster and correspondent).

FOREWORD

I am writing this in Moscow Airport, having read the manuscript of this book while waiting for a plane to London. I mention this because I have just been lecturing Russian politicians on how to live with journalists in a free society. If I had known then what is in this book, I would have given it to them. So much of it is of universal value to those whose fate is to be interviewed by journalists in this information age.

Diana Mather's book is all the better for emanating from the real world of Manchester and from a television professional who has no illusions about journalists. Indeed, it is refreshing to find another journalist unafraid to assert that her fellow practitioners are not inevitably clothed in white raiments.

She packs a lot of common sense born of hard experience into these pages. Not that I agree with every word of it. I would be fiercer in my advice about speaking to journalists. NEVER tell them anything you do not wish to see in print or hear broadcast.

However, whether or not I agree with Miss Mather in detail is not the point. You will not go far wrong if you follow her advice. My hope is that the book is read by businessmen and women who treat the media with disdain but fall apart when they cannot avoid newspaper, radio or television journalists. Their handling of all three is often abysmal.

The image of British commerce and industry would almost certainly improve if executives took to heart and practised Miss Mather's advice. At least they would think before speaking.

Sir Bernard Ingham

To Peter, for all his help, experience and encouragement.

*To Jane Graham-Maw, Michele Turney and everyone
at Thorsons.*

To my father, who didn't live to read this book.

chapter one

WHAT'S IT ALL ABOUT?

THE PRESS

Today's newspaper or magazine journalist lives in a different world from that of a few years ago. It is important to bear in mind that the press has been, and is, going through a tremendous period of change. Technology, competition and pressure on jobs all have an effect on how a journalist looks at you, your business and your story. A clampdown on spending means there are fewer people to do the same amount of work, and competition means that there is more pressure to be first with the story. It is perhaps more tempting for journalists trying to make their names to 'embroider' the story slightly to get it a bigger, better slot – although most journalists would deny this. First of all, though, it is important to look into the past to understand the present.

A Potted History

The press really became free with the repeal of 'the taxes on knowledge' in the middle of the nineteenth century. This meant economic emancipation from political control. The growth of profits from advertising meant that the press was no longer economically dependent on the state. In 1834, when *The Times* had more journalists and advertising than other papers, it announced that it would stop receiving early information from government offices because such a practice was not consistent 'with the pride and independence of our journal' (*The Times*, 26 December 1834). This led to more permanent and better-paid jobs rather than freelance and casual work. It seems the wheel has turned full circle, with journalists now often being employed on short-term contracts.

In Victorian times, many editors were the owners, or were related to the owners, of the paper. Lords Northcliffe and Beaverbrook exercised a great deal of personal control over the content of their papers. Indeed, Lord Beaverbrook said he ran the *Daily Express* 'merely for the purpose of making propaganda, and with no other motive'. He was a terrible hypochondriac, and was quite sure that because he was fascinated by every illness known to man, his readers would be too. He told the *Express*'s editor that 'the public like to know what diseases men die of ... and women too'. Lord Northcliffe owned the rival *Daily Mail*, and its readers were treated to his particular whims when it came to editorial content. He had an obsession with torture and death, so his staff were ordered to 'find one murder a day' (some things never change!). At times the control was so intrusive that editors were forced to resign. This conflict between owner and editor still occasionally rages today, and was most apparent in the *Daily Mirror* when it was owned by the late Robert Maxwell. Rupert Murdoch is another owner who exerts a powerful influence, but without the almost daily interference that drove Maxwell's editors to resign.

As the papers grew more powerful, the broadsheets put huge resources into their prime investigative units. They had a high tolerance for stories that did not make it, and this gave their journalists the time and encouragement to search for the 'big' story that would eventually hit the headlines. Nowadays, after the changes in ownership of many of the papers, much of the back-up (and the money) is no longer there. Newspapers no longer have quite the instant, dramatic effect they once had, and much of the serious investigative journalism has moved into the realms of television.

In the past, the classic route to Fleet Street for those who did not go to university was to work on a small weekly paper, progress to a larger regional weekly such as the *Liverpool Echo* or *Yorkshire Post* and then join the Manchester office of a national daily. Roy Greenslade, a former editor of the *Daily Mirror* under Maxwell, was a young reporter on *The Sun* at the end of the 1960s. He sees the main change in the attitude of the press starting in 1969 when Murdoch bought *The Sun*: 'A lot of people think of Rupert Murdoch as being the progenitor of what we now think of as the tabloid press, but at that time the world was changing dramatically. *The Sun* was cheeky and irreverent in the way the *Daily Mirror* had been cheeky and irreverent in the fifties.'

Certainly at the time when The Beatles and The Rolling Stones were hitting the headlines, the *Daily Mirror*'s reporters were older men who could not understand the explosion of youth culture. They poured scorn on the whole thing, thereby probably losing a generation of new young readers. They were still part of the establishment, and compared with today the press was terribly tame. There were lots of small newspapers and they were very cheap; quite often people would buy one in the morning and then another at lunchtime to keep themselves up to date. Now newspapers are much bigger, cost more and we read less, relying on radio and television to give us up-to-the-minute news.

National Press

The Tabloids
It is fair to say that the tabloid press as we know it today was born in Britain. Fierce competition coupled with rising costs and falling profit margins puts huge pressures on editors to

come up with more sensational material, and the British tabloid journalist is said to be the hungriest, meanest and fastest in the world. The thing guaranteed to sell papers is a big news event or sensational story, and journalists will do their best to outbid each other in order to get that 'scoop', which could increase circulation by as much as 200,000 to 300,000 copies. They will buy a big story even if it is not completely accurate, taking a shred of evidence and turning it into something that will hit the headlines. It does not have to be a new story either; the word 'recently' can mean as long ago as last year.

In the 1980s *The Sun*'s irreverence under Kelvin McKenzie became increasingly anti-establishment, which caught the mood of the Thatcher generation and set the trend for its rivals. Newspapers have groomed the public into believing that they have a right to know, and this has meant the growth of intrusion into the private lives of anyone in the public eye. Papers like *The Sun*, the *Mirror* and the *News of The World* look for the more sensational angle of the stories they print and often get criticized for it. They would say that we get the press we deserve, and certainly the general public is hypocritical at times.

Take the fuss over the printing of pictures taken of Princess Diana in the gym in 1993. The *Daily Mirror* did not commission the pictures; they were offered them for a sum of money. Was the *Mirror* right to publish? There was uproar and recrimination at the time, but the *Mirror*'s circulation rocketed. The more 'middle class' tabloids such as the *Mail* and *Express* would probably shy away from alienating their loyal (or loyalist!) readers, but they too concentrate on the human angle, and are as tenacious as their rivals when it comes to researching and gathering news.

If a story is really hot, journalists will sometimes go to absurd lengths to get the report, even if it means occasionally camping outside the house of an unfortunate member of the public for days on end. They will ring up at odd hours hoping to catch you off your guard and even pretend to sell you double-glazing in order to get into the house and do an interview! The large nationals have big budgets and can afford to pay handsomely for an exclusive deal, which can mean whole families being hidden away, safe from the clutches of rival papers.

The Broadsheets

The journalists working on the 'serious' papers do not go to these extreme lengths to sell their papers, and they are also more careful to check the accuracy and authenticity of their stories. Whereas tabloid journalists have traditionally worked their way up in the profession, the broadsheet reporters tend to have a university education, and the bias of their reporting is to educate as well as inform. However, they are all in the business of trying to get the angle on a story that will interest their readers most, thereby helping to sell the paper.

Any paper's political bent obviously affects the way a story is handled. During the railwaymen's strike in the 1980s, a journalist working on *The Daily Telegraph* was sent to get a story about railwaymen playing golf while they were supposed to be on strike. The story she came back with painted a very different picture: of a commitment to work, and wages that could not possibly pay for golf-club membership, even if the men had time to play. This was not the story the *Telegraph* wanted, and it was never printed.

Most journalists want to get at what they see is the truth. Working on the nationals, they are used to interviewing top people who in their turn are often highly experienced in dealing with the press, but even the most cynical hack finds it difficult to 'nail' an interviewee who is obviously nervous but eager to help, up-front and open. Never forget, though, that the most important qualifications for being a journalist are to be two-faced as well as a licensed nosy parker! Many journalists are extremely cynical because they feel they are (as one put it to me) 'fed so much rubbish'. A tip for young reporters from an American journalist is to look at someone and think 'Why is this bastard lying to me?'

Local Press

Local papers, too, have changed a great deal recently. First, they are much more dependent on advertising than before. Second, there have been huge changes since the 'hot-metal' days, as the journalist is now the writer, compositor and lay-out man as well as being the gatherer of news. Part of the regional journalist's job is making friends in the community, nurturing the contacts and helping to bring the money in. There is an enormous difference between local and national papers and the journalists who work on them. Local papers tend to find a formula that works and stick to it. They are happy for their readers to take a proactive role, and will often take well-presented articles unaltered if they are very busy, and they are even more likely to use them if accompanied by a good photograph.

David Parry-Jones is editor of the weekly *Chester Chronicle* and has worked on the paper for thirty years: 'People should trust their local paper. If the paper puts a foot wrong, people know where to find us. I know most of the people in business here in Chester, my relationship with them is very good, and I want to keep it that way.' He feels that the behaviour of some of the tabloids has soured relationships and made people wary of making contact even with their local press. This worries him, as he feels that part of the role of papers like his is to help local businesses, as well as to inform, entertain and act as a watchdog for its readers.

It is generally true that you can have a much greater degree of trust in your local reporter, especially if you get to know him or her; and any reputable journalist will take 'off the record' seriously once parameters are established. Journalists are aware that, if nobody trusted the press at all, vital sources of information would completely dry up. Always remember that most reporters need you as much as you need them.

Free-sheets

The term 'free-sheets' is used to describe newspapers funded by advertisements and delivered free into thousands of homes all over the country. The past few years have seen a real growth in the number being produced. They are often owned by weekly or daily newspapers and will frequently use the same interviews that were printed in those papers, but at a slightly later date. Their editorial content is much lower, with less emphasis on news or features. If you are already an advertiser, they will most probably print an article if you submit it.

As with all local papers, the subjects covered by free-sheets must be of local interest. If, however, you own a national company with thirty regional bases, these free-distribution newspapers could provide you with thirty outlets in which to publicize the group's activities.

Trade Press

There is a wealth of publications that report on almost every trade or industry. These can be extremely valuable as the articles are often picked up by the national papers. A good example is the case of Public Image, the company of which I am a partner. Around the time when television cameras were being introduced into the House of Commons, several MPs had contacted us asking for special training. We thought this would make a good article, so we approached our trade publication, *PR Week*. They interviewed us over the phone and printed a piece which was picked up by Jane

Thynne and made the front page of *The Daily Telegraph*. We were inundated with calls from journalists working for local and national papers, magazines, television and radio. We handled all sorts of interviews and appeared on all kinds of programmes. We are still in many journalists' contact books, so that if there are questions to be answered on image or interview training, they ring us first. You cannot buy that kind of publicity!

The trade magazines want interesting, factual articles. They are often read by the very people your company or organization wants to target most, so I would advise anyone to read the sort of articles that are published and decide whether you should be contacting the magazines that relate to you, either directly or through your public-relations agency. Journalists who work for the trade press should never be underestimated – although they ought to fight the corner for their particular industry, they will be critical if they feel it is necessary. Some of the journals are extremely influential, and even the ones that might only be of interest to a particular industry are frequently taken home by staff and read by the rest of the family. The editors will often take well-written press releases and reprint them in their entirety, as well as using good photographs of products or people.

Magazines

There are hundreds of magazines covering every hobby, sport, business and leisure activity you can think of. They are always on the look-out for ideas and stories, and provide a useful outlet to promote your product or service. They are also in the business, however, of getting as much advertising revenue as possible and will not give you a free commercial! Indeed, many magazines will only print an article if the company submitting it also takes advertising space. If you do advertise in the magazine, try to ensure that the advert is not placed near the editorial copy. If possible, get them to print the advert in the issue following your article so that you get two bites of the cherry.

If you are offering magazines something special, new or different they will want to hear from you. A friend of ours who is a craftsman had an article showing his work in 'House And Garden' magazine. When he went to discuss it with the editor, she asked him if he would be able to cope with the rush of orders that would follow the publicity. He is still coping! Be guided by the editor as to what the article should include, especially photographs, as they will want you and your product to look as good as possible.

Magazines usually have a 'house style', both for pictures and copy, so you have to fit in with them. Regional magazines, in common with most others, have a very long shelf life (think of the ones in the dentist's waiting room!) so your item could be read by a large number of people for quite a long time.

Press Agencies

There are several news agencies that supply information to papers, radio and television. Apart from coverage of Parliament, the Old Bailey and the High Court, they also cover sport, financial news and foreign affairs. Reuters is still one of the largest in the business, with well over 100 years experience. Not only does it supply foreign news to the media, it also provides a comprehensive economic service to British business, with up-to-the-minute reports directly into company's offices. If you have something newsworthy to say about your business, then the press agencies are only too happy to hear from you.

What to Ask a Press Journalist

There are crucial questions that should be asked when you are approached by anyone connected with the press:

- Why me?
- Who is the journalist?
- What is the story?
- Who else is being interviewed?
- What publication is the journalist from?
- What is the angle?
- Where do they want to carry out the interview?
- Who is the audience?

Having asked the journalist questions, you then have to ask yourself:

- What benefits will you or your organization gain from the interview?
- Are you the right person?
- Do both you and your company want to do it?

Let us look at those questions in more detail:

Why Me?
They will want to interview you because:

- You are the expert.
- The journalist, while looking through the cuttings library, sees you have been interviewed on the subject in the past.
- Somebody has given them your name.

Who Is the Journalist?

The next step is to find out who the journalist is and where he or she works. I have never worked for the *The Guardian*, but you would be surprised how many people would speak to me if I rang and said that I was writing a feature for them. Always check. Get a number and ring back. It may be that they are working from home, or are one of the growing number of freelancers who are employed these days, but if the paper they say they are working for has never heard of them, beware! Quite legitimately, the journalist may write the piece speculatively and then try and sell it, but if he or she is unable to place it, you could have wasted a couple of hours. You need to know who they are so that you can decide whether or not to speak to them.

If newspaper journalists ring out of the blue, never speak to them without giving yourself time to get your brain in gear. A good phrase to remember is 'stall – but call'. Tell them you are unable to talk to them at that moment; ask them briefly what they want and hang up. As most journalists are working to a deadline, do call back at the allotted time. During the ten minutes, half an hour or half a day before you have arranged to ring back, do as much research into the subject as you can. One tip is to ask them to fax you any relevant information, as this will give you extra time. You can never know how much information journalists have managed to glean, but one thing is sure – if there are any skeletons in your cupboard they will probably know about them! Bear in mind, however, that you are the expert in your field, with more knowledge at your fingertips than most journalists will ever have, except perhaps those who work in very specialized areas.

It is important to know the style of the journalist who is going to interview you. An interview for your local paper will be handled differently from one for a tabloid, and that in turn will be different from the more serious broadsheet. If someone is going to do a feature on you, ask them to send you a sample of their work.

What Is the Story?

To find out what the story is, it is important to know from where the idea originated. Ask the journalist. Once you know the source, try and find out as much as you can about the background. If it has been in a local paper, for instance, get hold of a copy. Libraries or the newspaper offices concerned will be able to oblige. It is essential to get as much information as possible before you talk to the journalist.

Who Else Is Being Interviewed?

You need to know. Editors often encourage journalists to 'get a row going' – 'Ring the vicar and tell him what the verger said about him, then ring the verger and tell him what the vicar said.' We all like to read about what 'so and so did to whom and why'! If possible, contact the other interviewees and find out what they have said to the journalist. If they are likely to oppose your views, then some careful thought should help you gauge their reaction.

What Publication Is the Journalist From?

What might make a column in *The Daily Telegraph* after an interview on the phone could be picked up and extended by the tabloid press, so it is important to establish who the journalist is writing for. Local papers and magazines often want photographs, so be prepared for a photographer to come with the reporter. Reporters from *The Times* may spend more time exploring background information, researching company reports etc. and having lunch with the directors of various organizations, while the journalists from *The Sun* will probably talk to as many people as possible who can throw light on the story and add the human element.

What Is the Angle?

The angle of the piece is not always determined by the reporter. He or she usually has a set agenda, and may or may not be prepared to tell you what it is, but they do not necessarily have the last word as far as the copy is concerned. That is down to the editor.

Where Do They Want to Carry Out the Interview?

Where does the reporter want to meet you, or are you going to chat over the phone? Where you arrange to meet journalists and the impression you create obviously has a bearing on how they write about you. If I lived in a splendid mansion, and was managing director of a company that had made a large part of its workforce redundant, I would make sure I was interviewed in the office! Whether it was true or not, the inference that could be drawn from the house is that the management is creaming off profits to subsidize a luxurious lifestyle.

Your house, garden, décor, possessions, what you read and what you wear all help the journalist to build up a picture of you. So without going to the trouble of redecorating the kitchen or buying a new wardrobe of clothes before a reporter walks through the door, think about the impression that you are making, both to the journalist and, through him or her, to the readers.

Who Is the Audience?

The broadsheet papers would present a different angle on a story than, for example, *Hello!* magazine, while the trade press will take a different stance from the tabloids. To do a good interview you have to know who the story is aimed at. The tabloid journalist will want details like the age of the people they are talking about, the price of their houses and the make of their cars as well as more sensational and sexy angles. These are not as important to the 'serious' papers, who will concentrate on the core of the story. Magazines want to interest their readers with a more general approach, often focusing on the glamorous aspects of the subjects' lives. Local papers need information that is relevant to the area covered by their circulation, and the trade press want to know the latest developments in the industry that their journal serves.

RADIO

BBC Network Radio

The British Broadcasting Corporation was formed in 1926, giving birth to the most prestigious and influential broadcasting organization in the world. Its mission is 'to educate, inform and entertain'. Through its Charter, the BBC is ultimately responsible to the government, and there are strict guidelines for journalists and producers. When Sir Robin Day joined in 1955, the BBC was still being run on the rather military lines imposed by Lord Reith. Radio was the senior service and current affairs went under the cosy title of 'Talks'. In his book *The Grand Inquisitor*, Sir Robin describes his first morning as a temporary producer. The welcome he received went something like this:

> Ah, Day! Good morning, welcome to 'Talks'. Now to give you some advice. I want you to see yourself as having become an officer in a rather good regiment. Please regard John Green as the Colonel as myself as the Adjutant. Do you follow? Now I expect you'd like some advice about dress? I see you're wearing a stiff collar? Well, you may be glad to know that here we do not insist on stiff collars, but in 'Talks' we like to wear suits. In features they wear sports jackets, and I have to

admit that in Drama they even wear corduroys. But, as
I say, in 'Talks' we like suits.

'Talks' has progressed into one of the most envied current-
affairs departments in the world, and it has seen a great many
changes since the days of the Home Service. In the early days,
newsreaders wore dinner jackets to read the news and everybody had to have 'an Oxford accent' even if they had never
been to Oxford! Nowadays the BBC actively encourages
regional accents, even for some of the newsreaders who present the main, nationwide news bulletins. The World Service,
too, has increased its coverage from purely news to drama,
features and current affairs. This fact should not be underestimated, as it means a thirty-second 'sound bite' might very
well be transmitted world-wide, thereby spreading your
message across the globe. The advent of Radio 5 Live has
broadened even more the amount of news and current affairs
that the BBC covers.

BBC Local Radio

The BBC used to be broken down into four English regions,
as well as the national ones for Scotland, Wales and Northern
Ireland. Alongside their purely regional output, they would
provide news, drama, features and light entertainment
which would be slotted into the national menu, operating in
much the same way that BBC regional television does today.
When the first BBC local radio stations were launched in the
1970s, the regions were disbanded. Many people wondered
whether this was a wise move – stretching already stretched
resources into the realms of what was virtually just community radio. BBC local radio has changed a lot since then. At
one time it used to try to ape its independent competition,
even poaching presenters from independent stations, a strategy that often confused the listeners. Now the accent is on

giving the listeners a choice, and the move in local radio is towards more speech rather than more music.

BBC local radio is a marvellous training ground for broadcast journalists as well as being the grass-roots news-gathering service for the whole of the BBC including World Service. It offers openings to individuals and companies who want to get involved with the media because the stations are always on the lookout for stories and features. Even though there is a now a pooling of resources through the syndica-tion of programmes over several stations (a return in part to the old, regional format), the drawback for the interviewee is that some reporters are either fresh from university or straight from a local paper, and you have no idea what expe-rience they have got until you are on the other side of the microphone! It throws the onus more on you to make sure they know the story that you are there to tell. Often they will appreciate all the information you can give them, because they want to produce an interesting and entertaining inter-view as much as you do. It is in nobody's interest to leave the listener more confused and less informed than they were to start with!

A big change in the BBC has been the Bi-Media policy. This means that in theory there is 'one BBC'. If you are inter-viewed by Radio Oxford, the item could be picked up by the *Today* programme and later make the national television news.

Independent National Radio

As yet there are few national, independent radio stations on the air. One recent success story has been Classic FM, which offers a mix of classical music as well as various arts-maga-zine programmes. For musicians, artists, actors and writers it can give welcome publicity to a concert, exhibition, play or publication. The style of interview is generally informal, encouraging the interviewee to make their particular subject interesting to as wide an audience as possible.

Independent Local Radio

During the recession, advertising revenue has fallen, and there are more and more stations on the air after a piece of the same cake. The move in ILR is for more music, leaving speech to the BBC. There is news on the hour, and some stations have news and current affairs programmes which concentrate on local and national issues.

Independent Producers

Since the Thatcher government stated that twenty-five per cent of radio and television programmes must be made by independent producers there has been a proliferation of companies trying to grab a piece of the action. To the listener the output will sound much the same, with perhaps a change of presenter hosting a tried-and-tested format. Some of the companies are based in the stations where the programme is transmitted while others have their own production offices. The 'ten-till-twelve' Saturday slot on BBC Radio 2, for example, is now produced by an independent company, but the features that made it a success for the BBC have remained the same.

Both the BBC and independent radio have strong editorial control to safeguard standards. Competition is very strong, and as pilot programmes on radio are relatively cheap to produce, you could be asked to take part in one by a company trying to win the contract for a particular series. Before you spend too much time on the project, find out if it has a realistic chance of success or whether the pilot is purely speculative.

What to Ask a Radio Journalist

- Why me?
- What is the story?
- Who is the journalist and where is he or she from?
- Who else will be on the programme?
- What is the angle?
- Where will the interview take place?
- Will the interview be recorded or live?
- How long will the broadcast interview be?
- Who is the audience?
- What is the first question?

Why Me?
Why you? Ask them! You should be the person who is the most knowledgeable about the subject that they are interested in. On the other hand, your name could have been given to a researcher because you were interviewed somewhere on a similar topic.

What Is the Story?
The ideas for many radio interviews are sparked off by articles in either local or national newspapers or press releases, because that is where journalists begin looking for news when they start their shifts. Newspaper articles always relate to an event that has happened recently which has had an impact on the community, be it local or national, although on closer inspection only fifty per cent are accurate enough to warrant further investigation. If you are promoting a new album, book or film, you will be asked on to the programme to talk about that, and the launch date will dictate the timing of the interview. You should be given an outline of the areas of questioning, but probably not a list of questions; this is because the journalist will not want you to be so 'off pat'

that the interview sounds as though it has been pre-rehearsed. If you are given a list, make sure you are prepared for the unmentioned question.

A ploy among some reporters is to give a list of four or five questions and then slip in an extra one that throws the poor interviewee completely! If the interview is pre-record-ed, do not let the interviewer start the tape until you have all the facts at you fingertips and have had time to formulate your answers and the points you wish to make.

Who Is the Journalist and Where Is He or She From?

The radio station and programme will tell you quite a lot about the journalist. If the reporter is from *You And Yours* or *PM*, the item will be of national interest. If the reporter is from a local station, then the accent will be on local issues. Sometimes this will mean looking at a story in detail, with all sorts of people being interviewed. Local news of any importance is sometimes thin on the ground, so when some-thing momentous happens, it is milked for all it is worth. A report that might make thirty seconds on the national news could make a ten-minute segment on a local news-magazine programme.

Who Else Will Be on the Programme?

Always ask who else will be contributing to the programme, and if there are plans to include any pre-recorded interviews. If there are, ask to hear them. If you are not given the chance, then listen carefully to the introduction of the piece and be prepared for the unexpected. Sometimes a very emotive interview from somebody with an opposite point of view can precede yours, and this will have set the scene in the listen-er's mind. Unless you are ready, it can throw you off course.

What Is the Angle?

By asking certain questions such as 'What are you looking

for?' or 'What do you see as the nub of this story?', you should be able to gain some idea of the angle the reporter is looking for.

Where Will the Interview Take Place?

Find out if they want you to go to the studios or whether the reporter will come and interview you at home or in your office. Be aware of your surroundings as they could influence the introduction to the item (*see chapter 7*). They could talk to you over the telephone, in which case it is as well to knock at least half an hour out of your schedule as these contributions often run late.

Will the Interview Be Recorded or Live?

Live interviews are the most exciting! It is most likely you will be in the studio, but quite a number of telephone pieces are also live. Always be sure to ask how long the interview is going to be, as this will give you some idea of the amount of information you can get across to the listeners.

How Long Will the Broadcast Interview Be?

If the interview is recorded, it is vital that you are told roughly how long the finished interview will last. It is no good talking for forty minutes if they are only going to use two-and-a-half! Try and find out exactly what angle they are looking for and aim your answers at that. When you feel you have said enough, thank them politely and finish. Do not be encouraged to say more than you are prepared for. It is very easy to be lulled into a false sense of security and forget there is a tape running if you become involved in the subject matter and get on well with the reporter.

Who Is the Audience?

Ask the producer or researcher who their audience is and at what sort of level you should pitch your answers. If in doubt, direct the answers to a lay audience, assuming they know very little. The message must be carefully thought out, however, as any hint of talking down or patronizing will have listeners reaching for the off button quicker than anything.

What Is the First Question?
Finding this out will give you an insight into the direction the interview will take.

TELEVISION

The BBC

Even when I joined the BBC in 1981, life was a lot more reliable than it is there now. Most people at the 'Beeb' were 'staff', and you had to do something pretty horrendous to get the sack. If people were not quite up to the job, they were usually moved sideways to another department; in fact the BBC was said to be a company playing musical chairs, but instead of removing a chair, they put another one in! While this obviously helped to create some of the problems that we see in the Corporation today, there was a sense of pride and loyalty then that is now disappearing as fast as jobs. The BBC was the training ground for not only many of the world's top journalists and broadcasters, but also for the boffins and engineers who produced brilliant programmes on meagre resources. We were paid much less than ITV companies in those days, but motivation and job security made up for the lack of cash. When I first started reading the Northwest News I did not even have a contract; it was all done on a handshake.

Before the Bi-Media policy adopted in the early 1990s, resources were not shared as they are today. In the Regions there were different newsrooms for regional television and local radio, which meant using more journalists, copy-takers and equipment. There was no feeling of working together, and the BBC might have been four separate organizations. It was not unknown to see three or four BBC reporters at the scene of a major story: one television crew from the region where the incident took place, one crew from the national news and two radio reporters – one local and one national. That has all changed now.

In the early 1960s, news crews were much bigger and the equipment more cumbersome. A typical crew would comprise a reporter, director, cameraman, sound recordist and at least one sparks (electrician), the same size crew as is now used for documentary programmes. Nowadays the news crew consists of a reporter, camera operator and usually a sound recordist. The reporter and camera operator between them decide the angle – of the story and the shot. The news-readers have changed too. When television news was first broadcast the readers were unseen, a voice behind still photographs. The first 'on-screen' readers were recruited from the world of drama or even industry, not from journalism as they are today.

With the growth of technology where satellite link-ups are possible from almost anywhere in the world, the pressure is on to be first. Problems arise when there is not enough time to double-check the story, and some reporters will say that accuracy can be at risk, something that has to borne in mind when talking to journalists. The onus is on you to make sure they have accurate facts at their fingertips – if they do, there is every chance they will use them! In the 1980s we saw the number of national news bulletins increase and more resources were put into the Regions to give an equally wide coverage. The BBC is also investing in more specialist reporters. Again, this could present opportunities for you or your organization.

BBC 2

BBC 2 was originally set up to promote minority-interest programmes, specialist documentaries, some sport and the arts.
The programme budgets are smaller as the audience is not
as large as that for most of the output on BBC 1. It is also the
place where programmes can be tested before going into the
prime-time slots.

Independent Television

When commercial television first came on the air, it was said
by some to be a licence to print money! This new form of
advertising took off in a big way, and the new ITV companies were able to pay top rates for top people on both sides
of the camera, who were recruited from the world of film or
from the BBC. The offers were lucrative and the atmosphere
very different. The new companies were owned by showmen
such as Val Parnell and the Grade brothers. Their first priority was to win the audience, and they took little notice of
critics of their style of broadcasting, one of whom wanted
'more cultural programmes and less airy frolics'. They left
'culture' to the BBC.

The choice of area was also geared to the advertisers. It is
said that one reason that Sidney Bernstein, the founder of
Granada Television, chose Manchester for his region was
'because it has the highest rainfall in England'. He reckoned
that more people would therefore stay indoors and watch
television. Because of the sponsors, it was vital for ITV that
programmes went on the air and attracted viewers who
would stay tuned and watch the commercial breaks.

The ITV unions became all-powerful, especially the electricians. They could, and did, hold companies to ransom –
all they had to do was turn off the lights! They managed to
win all sorts of concessions that we poor performers (especially freelancers) could never hope for. A good example of

this was the fact that the unions could insist that crews work-ing on an outside broadcast had to be offered a choice of three different menus for lunch or dinner. To ensure a substantial nosh, at least one had to include gravy!

Overnight stays in hotels and fees for 'disruption', even when travelling a distance of, say, forty miles, all added to the cost of programmes, and overtime was paid at up to three or four times the hourly rate. There was one occasion, at a political party conference, when the prime minister of the day received a standing ovation, apparently to his mild sur-prise. The applause was started by some electricians, driven more by opportunism than political fervour. They had seen the time was two minutes to one. If the transmission went on beyond one o'clock, their meal break would be infringed, earning them extra money. As the PM sat down, they stood up, clapping loudly until the rest of the hall followed suit. By the time he had taken a few bows the clock had ticked past one o'clock. This meant NLB (no lunch break) and an hour's overtime, simply because the break had not started at one on the dot. The fact that the crew's lunch hour lasted from two minutes past one until two minutes past two was neither here nor there! These sort of excesses cost the indus-try dear, and obviously things had to change. Change they certainly have. Nowadays, most crews have to work a ten-hour day before they get a penny in overtime, and some are lucky to get any lunch at all!

The pressures on ITV stations have been far greater since they have had to tender for their franchises. Some companies pay up to fifty-five million pounds each year for the privi-lege of broadcasting; while others, who were unopposed, pay only a few thousand. Because there are shareholders to sat-isfy, the budgets for production have been cut, and many companies are looking for cheaper ways to fill the air-time. One of those ways, apart from showing cheap American imports, is to use audience-participation shows. This has greatly increased access for members of the general public and representatives of all manner of industrial, professional and special-interest groups to get involved and be both seen and heard in the many regional and national talk shows.

Channel 4

Channel 4 was set up to make specialized programmes and documentaries not in the mainstream of popular entertainment – the ITV equivalent of BBC 2. As well as commissioning its own programmes, it also buys in from ITV companies and independent producers who send in programme ideas. The commissioning editors get a mountain of programme treatments to read every week, and the competition for selection is extremely fierce.

Cable and Satellite

The growth of cable and satellite television and the increasing number of broadcasting hours available has also changed the scene. These hours have to be filled with news and current-affairs programmes as well as quiz shows and Australian soaps, but as there is only a certain amount of money, the use of inexperienced journalists is on the increase. The size of the station will determine the number of staff they employ and therefore how much research is done. In a small station you can get to know the journalists and build up a relationship with them; often they will be very pleased to look at any ideas you may put forward.

Satellite television tends to take a similar angle to that of the tabloid newspapers. The channels need to get viewers for their sponsors, and the emphasis is on entertainment and the need to appeal to a mass audience. British Sky Broadcasting is the biggest satellite station transmitting from the UK at the moment. They employ experienced presenters for their news and current-affairs programmes, and the interviews are often longer than their terrestrial equivalents. The planning time for their features can be anything up to two months, depending on the availability of the camera crews and production staff. There are satellite channels devoted to shopping, children, movies, leisure and 'lifestyle' activities. These can provide useful promotional opportunities for products and people. The cable channels are sometimes short-lived, and their audience is limited by the size of their allotted area. Both satellite and cable stations are also a training ground for journalists and production staff, who tend to move quite frequently once they have gained some experience.

Independent Television Producers

At first, many of the independents were made up of producers from the BBC or ITV who took early retirement and started their own companies and submitted ideas. Some programmes that were originally produced by the major broadcasting organizations became independent productions themselves, such as *Kilroy!*, while others, such as Granada's *This Morning*, take 'strands' – features that are produced independently.

The format has now broadened to include producers and directors who have never worked in broadcast television, often coming from the world of corporate videos. The standard of production varies on the experience of the personnel involved. One problem is that the budgets are often smaller, which means there is less time devoted to the project; the other is that there are many companies bidding for each programme and the competition is ferocious. You could be approached by a hopeful company to prepare material or even record a pilot programme without any guarantee that it will ever be made or transmitted. Before you spend too much time working on a project, it is as well to enquire about its prospects; on the other hand, the experience of doing dummy interviews or working in front of a camera is extremely valuable.

What to Ask a Television Journalist

- Why me?
- What is the story?
- Where is the journalist from?
- Who else will be on the programme?
- What is the angle?
- Where will the interview take place?
- Will the interview be recorded or live?
- How long will the broadcast interview be?
- Who is the audience?
- What do I wear?
- Do I need make-up?
- What is the first question?

Why Me?
Ask yourself why you have been contacted as well as asking the journalist. The same checklist applies as for radio (*see page 18*): am I the right person? What will be gained by myself or my organization from appearing on the programme?

What Is the Story?
Do not assume that the reporter will necessarily have the same facts on a story that you have. Ask them as many relevant questions as you can think of, so that if their information is wrong you can correct it. Make sure you talk through the main points of the interview before the cameras start rolling. Again, you should be given the area of questioning (*see page 29*). It is in the researcher's, reporter's or presenter's interest to give you as much help as is feasible so

that your performance will be relaxed, informative and interesting to their viewers.

Where Is the Journalist From?

What programme do they want you to appear on? Is it a news item, a documentary, a regional magazine programme or a talk show?

Who Else Will Be on the Programme?

Finding out who else is on the programme will help your preparation. Are there any pre-recorded pieces, film clips or interviews with the public (vox pops)? A poignant piece showing a woman walking her dog on a beautiful stretch of land that is about to be covered in concrete will certainly precondition the viewer's mind before you have had the chance to say a word.

Where Will the Interview Take Place?

Will the interview take place in a studio? Is a camera crew going to come to the office, and if so, how long will they be there? What image should you or the company project?

Will the Interview Be Recorded or Live?

Will the interview be pre-recorded? What time should you get to the studio? How long will you be there?

How Long Will the Broadcast Interview Be?

It can be dangerous to talk for forty minutes in a pre-recorded interview if the broadcast item is only going to last for two or three minutes. You could be lulled into a false sense of security and say something in an unguarded moment, and you will probably be unhappy with the edited version. Keep an eye on the time the interview starts, and when you feel you have said enough, thank the reporter politely and stop talking. Do not be drawn to say more. There are no strict rules as to how long it takes to record an interview, that depends on the journalist, but if it lasts for about fifteen or twenty minutes, that should be sufficient for them to get enough for an item of two or three minutes in duration. If the interview is live, ask how long it is likely to be so that you can begin to formulate your answers accordingly.

What Is the Angle?

If, when you ask the question, the answer seems a bit evasive – watch out! Most journalists, however, will give you as much information as you ask for, especially for a television or radio programme, because they want you to be able to tell their audience as much as possible about whatever it is you are there to talk about.

Who Is the Audience?

Again, it brings us to the vital question – the audience. When talking to anyone, whether it is at a conference, a departmental meeting or to the media, you must always know who you are addressing. It is not just a question of what you need to tell them, but of what they need to know. Ask the reporter, then think about the time of the day the programme will be transmitted as well as the subject matter. This will help you prepare the points you want to make as well as enabling you to predict some of the questions.

What Do I Wear?

The type of programme, the time of day, and the style of presentation will determine the clothes to wear. Always ask the producer or researcher what they think would be appropriate. For more information, *see chapter 2*.

Do I Need Make-up?

For most people the answer is yes! Lighting can drain the colour and texture from a face, leaving you looking pale or insipid. Do not forget that you will be judged against the presenter of the programme who will have had the benefit of make-up, so find out if there will be a make-up artist available. If not, some translucent powder and a comb can work wonders.

What Is the First Question?

(See page 21.)

CONCLUSION

The benefits of handling the media successfully are enormous, and the pitfalls can be costly. The greatest defence against disaster is to understand where the media are coming from, what their objectives are, and as far as possible to get them on your side in presenting a comprehensive and interesting story. The most important thing is to be yourself and try to enjoy what should be a stimulating and rewarding experience.

chapter two

THE INTERVIEW

What is an interview worth? The answer to that question varies a great deal depending on the programme and content of the interview, but there is an interesting calculation to be made. Although it would not be in anyone's best interests for you to try to convert an interview into a commercial for your cause, commercials do provide us with an interesting benchmark of value. A three-minute television commercial to be shown at peak time could easily cost around £100,000 a minute to produce. Since many television interviews fill three minutes of screen time, it could be argued that you are being given up to £300,000 as a gift! That sounds a wonderful, and indeed it can be – if handled well. The bad news is that if handled wrongly, that asset will turn into an equally powerful liability, so you need to prepare. Never attempt an interview unless you are sure of the subject. Vanity is what makes most people say 'yes' to a media interview. However in most cases, handled properly, it will do you or your organization no harm at all to raise your profile.

THE PROS AND CONS

There are pros and cons to be weighed, so let us look at the factors for and against getting involved.

The plus points of the interview could include:

- It is good for public relations.
- It gives free promotion.
- It raises your company profile.
- It boosts staff morale.
- It makes your name with the media.
- It gives you a chance to prevent or correct mistakes or misunderstandings.
- It gives you the opportunity to target a specific audience.
- It provides interview experience.

And the negative points of taking part could be:

- The timing could be bad (for the company, stock market, staff, shareholders etc.).
- There might be no time to prepare.
- You might not be the right person to take part.
- You could be in a no-win situation.
- It could be better to let the media attention die down.
- There could be a threat to your career.
- You do not want to be made to look foolish.
- Your views could be misrepresented.

Only you can balance the arguments for and against your participation, and they need careful thought. If you think it is important for your organization or company to take part in the programme, but you are not the right person, give the journalist the name of the relevant individual after you have discussed it with him or her.

THE CONTACTS BOOK

It is a good idea to make a note of the names and numbers of journalists who have interviewed you in the past. If the articles they wrote were to your liking, make a point of keeping in touch so that you can tell them if a possible story crops up. Think, too, about contacting those whose work covers your area, whether they work for the press, magazines, radio or television.

It is always difficult to know how far to go when approaching journalists. They will not be 'bought' with too much hospitality or extravagant corporate gifts. There is an old saying: 'the better the lunch, the worse the story!' Lunches should be used for making and maintaining friendships, putting faces to names and swapping gossip, not for announcing hard news. Like any chief executives, newspaper editors are very busy, but as they set the tone of their papers, any chance of meeting them should be taken. If you find that you cannot entice them out for lunch, make sure they are on the invitation lists for events such as trade association or shareholders' meetings. It is also useful to make a note of journalists who have written adversely about you or your profession, so that at least you are forewarned if they contact you in the future.

JARGON

Avoid using jargon. Nothing alienates an audience quicker than using short-forms they do not understand or cannot identify with – the verbal shorthand you might use to communicate with someone who knows your industry or profession. If you are going to use acronyms, make sure you explain them to begin with.

Here are some journalistic terms that may be useful to understand when discussing an interview with a reporter.

On and Off the Record

Some people say the rule about talking 'off the record' is quite simple. Do not do it unless it is with someone you know well and have learned to trust over a long period – like your mother! Unless it is stressed, assume that everything you say is on the record and may be used against you. There are times, however, when you need to help the journalist understand a story, but do not want what you say to be printed. It is necessary then to tell them firmly that it is 'off the record'. Most reputable journalists will abide by this unwritten rule, and the reporters with whom you are in regular contact will co-operate, as it helps them to have as much background information as possible. Some people, though, have been badly let down, and I suppose the only safe thing is to say nothing that you are not going to be happy to see in print. Do not take anything for granted.

Sir Bob Scott is no stranger to any branch of the media as head of the Manchester Olympic Bid Committee in 1993. One of the things he learnt was the difference between being interviewed by radio and by the press. Over the period that Manchester competed to bring the Games to Britain, Bob got to know some press journalists very well. Both he and they knew instinctively when things were on and off the record. In the course of one interview with a radio reporter, however, he expressed some thoughts about why the bid had been lost. Out of this substantial interview the journalist used only a couple of sentences, the ones that related adversely to the two British International Olympic Committee members. Bob had momentarily forgotten the difference between a conversation with a radio reporter and a conversation with a journalist using a notebook. It is up to you to do your own editing on radio, whereas the newspaper journalist will often assist you. If anything is to be said off the record to a broadcast journalist, make sure it is said before the tape starts running!

Non-attributable

If you want to give information to a journalist, but do not want to be named, then make sure he or she understands that it is non-attributable. That means the journalist can use what you have said but not reveal who said it.

Embargo

An embargo requires that, although a piece of information has been given to journalists, they are not allowed to publish it in any form until a specified date or time. If you are sending out a press release, put the words 'Embargoed until ...' in bold type at the top of the page. If you are speaking to journalists, make sure they realize the date and time of the embargo. Embargoes are seldom broken because they are a useful way for journalists to gather early information, and it is not in their interest to break that trust.

Leak

The technique of leaking news to one journalist in order to arouse the curiosity of others is an old one. It is regularly used by government and politicians who want to test the reaction to measures that might prove controversial.

Exclusive

All branches of the media love an exclusive! It means that they are first with the story. It not only gets people talking about the story itself, but also about the paper or programme that carries it. The only problem with the exclusive is that you may obtain maximum publicity from one source, but very little from any others.

Doorstepping

Doorstepping is what happens when you are confronted by hordes of journalists when leaving the house or office. There is no point in trying to avoid them, as an undignified view of your beam-end as you retreat hastily back indoors does not do an awful lot for your image. If you are in the middle of a 'hot' story, it is likely the journalists will want to talk to you about it. It can be most off-putting to have to face an unruly mob all firing questions at the same time, so decide what you are going to say before you go out and face them. If you have concluded a meeting and several people are leaving at the same time, elect a spokesperson. Say what you have to say and try not to get drawn into answering questions. If you do take questions, select the one you want to answer, answer it and then thank the journalists politely and walk firmly to your car or back into the building.

Stringer

Stringer is the term used for freelance journalists who send in copy to the papers in the hope that it will be used. Sometimes they are paid a retainer by one or more of the larger papers, with extra money if the items are used. Others are self-employed and will sell stories to any paper or broadcasting station that will pay for them, often using different styles for different papers. To get copy into a paper, the reporter sometimes has to apply a bit of 'top-spin'. A reception to herald a big initiative launched in Manchester was being covered by the national dailies, so the freelance journalist attending had to find a different slant to get his story into the papers. Talking to people failed to give him an angle, but he noticed that the promotional tee-shirts were made in Ireland, rather than what was the cotton capital of the world, Manchester. The heading 'Tee-shirts to promote Cotton City made abroad' got the piece into the papers, so the reporter got paid. Although there were a few red faces, it still got the project publicity, which in the end is what it is all about.

Regional journalists are as anxious as you to get a story into the nationals. A good way to gain publicity, if you think you have something of nationwide interest, is to offer the story to your local paper and hope that it will be taken up.

Soundbite

This is a phrase or sentence that the editor or reporter picks out of an interview to sum up what the story is all about. If you can encapsulate your message in a sentence, then that is the one that will be used if time is short. It may also be included in later bulletins where there may not be time to go into the story in detail. Journalists love soundbites!

Wires

This is a term left over from the days when news was sent by telegraph. A number of agencies are linked directly into newsroom computer systems, acting as a constant source of news from Britain and around the world.

Down the Line

This is the term used to describe an interview taking place over the phone or from a satellite studio.

Sub Judice

If someone has been charged with a criminal offence, the matter becomes what is called sub judice. This means it cannot be commented on outside the confines of the court without incurring the risk of proceedings for contempt. You can go to jail for this.

MISREPRESENTATION

Many people feel they are misrepresented or misquoted by the media. It is so easy to forget how what you say can be taken out of context. Reporters may be asking you questions simply to gain more information, but they could be leading you on. If, for instance, they stop asking direct questions, but suggest a summary, such as: 'Would you say then, that as protesters have delayed the planning appeal, the by-pass will be shelved?' It could be that you generally agree with what was said, but if you answer 'Yes', the article in the paper on the following day could read 'Mr Smith, head of the council's Planning Committee, said yesterday that the activities of protesters had effectively put paid to any plans for the long-awaited by-pass.'

If possible, do not answer a closed question with a direct response, because even a positive denial can lead to a story being printed. For example, if a journalist poses the question 'Do you think Councillor Thomas is guilty of fraud?' and you answer 'No', the journalist can print 'Mr Smith denied that Cllr. Thomas was guilty of fraud.' The question of fraud may not have been raised until this point, and you would be seen as the person who brought it up. The safe answer to that sort of leading question is: 'Cllr. Thomas is a conscientious, honest man who has spent the past five years serving the community.'

Unfortunately, misrepresentation is not always down to the reporter. A young journalist told me of an incident involving the Olympic gymnast Suzanne Dando. Suzanne was doing a series of interviews promoting fish, and the journalist was all set to do an article on eating fish as part of a healthy lifestyle. When asked about her family, Suzanne said that her marriage had broken up because her husband did not want children, but she did not want to talk about her private life. The reporter, having sympathy for her, wanted to respect this. When, however, the reporter returned to the offices of her regional evening paper, she was given a directive by the sub-editor turning the story completely on its head with the headline: 'My Secret Sorrow – wanting children wrecked Suzanne's life.' She was also told to mention fish only in the last paragraph, if at all! So even though you may be able to trust the reporter, you cannot trust an editor not to present the story in a way that will interest the paper's readers most. The lesson is, try to avoid mentioning anything that will draw the journalist's attention away from the story you want to tell.

MAKING A STATEMENT

The question of whether you should take part in a programme needs weighing up carefully. If you feel you are in a no-win situation, or that to take part in a interview would prolong adverse publicity, then it is better to prepare a positive statement that will put your case as succinctly as possible. The statement must, however, be very carefully thought out.

One instance of a statement backfiring happened during a Channel-4 documentary on solicitors who had been accused of acting with impropriety. One of the solicitors in question had to decide whether or not he should agree to be interviewed for the programme. After a great deal of thought, he decided not to take part as he had acted perfectly properly throughout the alleged case. The programme went ahead, on which a small part of his prepared statement was read out. This distorted the nuance of what he had actually said, making him seem uncaring and rather selfish. Make sure your statement says exactly what you want it to say, will stand up on its own and is impossible to edit. A cliché will not do, but a carefully constructed sentence will. Many large corporations feel that the pressure groups have the edge on them, as they put out short, succinct statements that are often used to close a report. Although they may not cover all the facts, they sound good.

A phrase for the chemical industry might be: 'The quality of life that we have all come to expect, depends on our products.' Or for the construction industry: 'Without a healthy construction industry, jobs and progress would be at risk.'

If a television company is going to use a photo to accompany your statement, make sure you send them a recent one that portrays the right image. Otherwise you could find they have used something from the library that may not be as flattering as you would wish!

How to Treat the Journalist

Try to treat the journalist in the same way you would treat a client or customer. You are, after all, trying to sell them your story, latest work or point of view. Try not to be late;

reporters have to meet deadlines, so if they have to rush, the information they print may not be as accurate as you would like. If you want their full attention do not ring them as they are meeting those deadlines (usually around three o'clock on a Thursday afternoon for weekly publications).

All journalists have a 'bullshit detector' that is immediately switched on when confronted by pomposity or eccentric behaviour. Joanna Coles, who writes a column in *The Guardian*, recalls interviewing a man in a restaurant who pretended he knew all the waiters. When he asked for 'his usual', the barman had no idea what he meant. Obviously this coloured the way she wrote the article as it showed a side of the man's character she had not realized was there. This sort of behaviour is a godsend to any journalist and can add a touch of spice to an otherwise bland story, so be as natural as you can.

Make sure the journalist has all your relevant details and knows who you are! A friend of mine who presents a radio breakfast show had an unnerving experience recently. There was an item about the Gas Board's latest price rises. The interviewee was shown into the studio by an harassed producer. The presenter read the introduction and asked the first question: 'Can you tell me why the Gas Board has decided on these latest round of price rises'? The rather urbane man thought for a minute and said 'Well, there's a lot of expensive equipment to buy, a lot of men to pay.' Presenter: 'That's as may be, but why now?' The man looked at the presenter again and scratched his chin. 'Christmas coming up, bonuses, all that sort of thing.' Presenter: 'Can you tell me if there are any more increases in the pipeline?' The man looked at him and said 'I don't think I can answer that.' By this time, patience was at a premium. Presenter: (with a steely edge to his voice) 'If I may take you back. First you say there's expensive equipment to buy and men to pay, then you don't know why the price is going to rise at this particular time, and when I ask if there are any price rises in the near future you are not prepared to tell me. May I ask you why?' The man looked him straight in the eye and said 'Perhaps it's because I'm a brain surgeon.' Which he was! A brain-surgery piece was coming up in the programme, and the doctor was a legitimate interviewee in the wrong slot. Such is the pace, particularly in the early morning, that some bizarre misunderstandings can arise, so if in doubt, write your name and title on a small piece of paper and hand it to the presenter as you go into the studio.

A good interview is a conversation that elicits information. In his book *The Grand Inquisitor*, Sir Robin Day reveals some of the guidelines he used when training reporters to interview for television thirty years ago. Some of them still hold good today, but unfortunately you cannot rely on all journalists being so professional or well-mannered:

- The television interviewer must do his duty as a journalist, probing for facts and opinions.
- He should set his own prejudices aside and reflect various opinions, disregarding probable accusations of bias.
- He should not allow himself to be overawed in the presence of a powerful person.
- He should not compromise the honesty of the interview, by omitting awkward topics or by rigging questions in advance.
- He should resist any inclination in those employing him to soften or rig an interview so as to secure a 'prestige' appearance, or to please Authority; if after making his protest, the interviewer feels he cannot honestly accept the arrangements, he should withdraw.
- He should not submit his questions in advance, but it is reasonable to state the main areas of questioning. If

he submits specific questions beforehand he is powerless to put any supplementary questions which may be vitally needed to clarify or challenge an answer.

- He should give fair opportunity to answer questions, subject to the time limits imposed by television.
- He should never take advantage of his professional experience to trap or embarrass someone unused to television appearances.
- He should press his questions firmly and persistently, but not tediously, offensively, or merely in order to sound tough.
- He should remember that a television interviewer is not employed as a debater, prosecutor, inquisitor, psychiatrist or third-degree expert, but as a journalist seeking information on behalf of the viewer.

KNOWING WHO YOUR AUDIENCE WILL BE

The time and style of the programme on radio or television will tell you a lot about your audience, and therefore the interview. If it is a breakfast show, people are generally busy shaving, making the tea, getting the children ready for school or dashing off to work. They are not giving you their full concentration. Listening to the radio in the car is the same; it is hoped that at least fifty per cent of the mind is on the road! This means that whatever you say has got to be succinct and to the point.

The make-up of that audience is likely to be different depending on the programme. *The Big Breakfast* on Channel 4 is aiming at a younger group than *GMTV* on ITV. The BBC's *Breakfast News* is competing for the same audience as the *Today* programme on Radio 4, as well as *Sunrise* on Sky.

Always try and watch or listen to the programme you are being asked to take part in; get somebody to record it if you are not at home when it goes out. It is important to get to know the style of the programme; how detailed is the interview likely to be? Is the slant more on entertainment or news?

The 'Hard' or Critical Interview

The critical interview is what people fear most, but often it is one of the easiest to handle, providing you are properly prepared. This type of confrontational interview is greatly enjoyed by some people, mainly politicians who are experienced in the art of debate as well as handling the media. The adrenalin flows and it is rather like a tennis match. When the balls are coming hard and fast, you only have to have your racket in the right place and the balls fly back over the net. If the line of questioning is not really going anywhere, and the ball barely bounces over the net, then you are pounding round the court, making all the running.

An interview should extract information, and there should be straight dealing with the people who are being interviewed. It should never give the impression, however, that the interviewer and interviewee have a cosy conspiracy and have decided in advance not to include certain topics. If the audience suspects the interview is all a bit of a game, there is no point in doing it. If, on the other hand, the line of questioning strays into areas you did not want to mention, say so. It is quite within your rights. There have been many cases of lack of liaison between researcher, producer and interviewer, resulting in questions being asked which the interviewee did not expect and is either unable or unwilling to answer. The resulting embarrassment can lead to accusations of dishonesty, or even worse, a half-baked attempt to answer the question, usually unconvincingly. This is not in anybody's best interests. If there are issues you do not want to touch on, make sure the reporter knows about them.

People who try to negotiate terms for interviews do not get very far. In most interviews of a critical nature journalists will try to get interviewees to say the one thing they do not want to say. They do this by using a certain amount of cunning, luring interviewees into a tight corner from which they cannot escape until they discuss the one topic they most wanted to avoid. Sometimes the journalist will try to embarrass you into it with questions like: 'I know you know the answer to my question, so why won't you tell us?' (The Paxman technique!) If you are attacked, the answer is to stay calm. If you are asked the same question again and again, you can say very politely: 'I have answered that question three times, and I'm afraid your viewers are going to get very bored, but I will answer it again,' and continue to give the same answer.

In a hard interview some presenters use the 'interviewer's nerve', a well-known ploy. It consists of the interviewer listening sympathetically, maybe even nodding kindly and saying nothing when you stop talking. He or she will look you steadily in the eye, giving you the impression of being riveted by what you are saying. The expression will say: 'Surely you've not finished. It's absolutely marvellous. Do go on.' If you do, you could find yourself in trouble. Resist the temptation to break the silence. The pause may last a second or two (although the first time the ploy is tried on you it will feel like a lifetime). Do not be embarrassed. Return the interviewer's kindly gaze and keep your mouth shut. The ball is in his or her court and has to be returned.

Press journalists also try to get you to say something that you will later regret. Reporters know that taking notes in front of people inhibits them, so, like policemen, they train themselves to make a mental note of what is said – and then transcribe it into the notebook afterwards, in the car or the pub. Just because the notebook is put away, do not assume the interview has finished.

However difficult the interview, always listen to, and answer, the questions. If you try and fudge, your interviewer might retaliate with: 'Very good answer, but I wonder if you would now like to answer my question?' This can be pretty undignified and sets the viewer or listener immediately on the side of the interviewer and against you. From then on, everything you say will have less impact. If the interviewer has got you on the spot, admit it, or as much as you want to admit: 'I've got to agree there's a lot in what you say. We have made mistakes in the past, but we've learnt from them and will do our best to make sure they won't happen again.' This sort of reply quite often throws interviewers off the trail. It can make them feel satisfied that they have been proved right, which means they will move on to another subject, leaving more sensitive issues untouched. Added to which, you have shown yourself as honest to the viewers! But do not depend on this strategy – the really sharp presenter will spot that you have told only half the truth and will continue to press for the whole story. It is important not to appear to the viewers to be evading the point. Do not forget that the oldest trick in the book is honesty, which is invincible, and it is usually possible to select a safe strand of argument and stick to it.

Preparing for the Questions

If, for instance, you run a construction company that is applying for planning permission to excavate a new quarry, and the other interviewees are from the local council and an environmental group, it is likely that the line of questioning will cover:

- Increased traffic – safety hazards, particularly to children.
- Narrow roads.
- Employment.
- Noise.
- Adverse affects on the environment.
- The length of time the land will be quarried.
- The need to quarry it in the first place.
- What will happen to the land when the quarrying has finished.
- Any antagonistic publicity about the firm in the past.
- The firm's safety record.

If you think round, inside, outside and through the subject, you should be able to anticipate the line of questioning.

If you are promoting a new book, album, exhibition or a theatrical or sporting tour, the question areas could include:

- The story or theme.
- The people to whom will it appeal.
- The cost.
- When the work is published or released.
- How long it will run.
- Who stars in it.
- How long has it taken to write, compile, rehearse etc.
- Your past performance.
- Your private life!

Sometimes journalists will not ask you the very question that would put everything you want to say in context, as this enables them to keep the story running for that little bit longer. The way to cope with this is to volunteer as much information as you can, including the answer to the unasked question.

No Comment

It is important to avoid the 'no comment' syndrome which tends to sow seeds of doubt in the minds of your audience. Provided you have done the necessary preparation, it is almost always better to say something, even if it is in a statement. One thing is sure, the boost to a company's morale from seeing their chief executive perform well on television is enormous and should not be underestimated!

The First Impression

It is said that you never get a second chance to make a first impression, and I think that's certainly true as far as the media is concerned. The first thing that we notice about someone on television is their face and hair. If you are a cabinet minister and you've had a few late nights and early starts before an interview, it's important that you don't look pasty-faced and tired. Apart from vanity, it can sow seeds of doubt in the voters' minds as to your fitness (both physical and mental) to do the job you have been elected to do. Looking fit and well is important for anyone, that's where a spot of make-up can come in very handy! Again, this may sound trivial, but if untidy hair, a drawn face or a crooked tie takes the viewer's concentration away from what you are saying, that expensive gift, that three hundred thousand pounds, is slipping away. Making a positive impression is much more difficult if someone looks dull and uninteresting, and this could have an impact on the product or service they are trying to promote. How can a book or play be really riveting if the author or director doesn't look and sound enthusiastic about it?

The image that is created by television has a huge effect on the impression of the interview. Sue Stapely is Press and

Parliamentary Officer for the Law Society in England and Wales. Her department has been trying to change the image of the 'dusty, old-fashioned lawyer' for some time now, and she feels dress and location are very important. 'Whenever a TV crew come to Chancery Lane they always want to film us standing in front of rows of ancient legal tomes wearing the most sober clothes we possess, which doesn't give a true reflection of the profession today.' Sue tries to make sure that the more modern offices are used as often as possible, showing computers on the desks with young fashionably dressed people hard at work. It sounds trifling but we all have our preconceptions of industrialists, politicians and professionals, and these have to be borne in mind when appearing on a programme.

What to Wear

The next thing we notice about people are their clothes. It is very important to dress in a way that reflects your image. That image may change for different programmes. The style of the programme dictates the style of dress, so take a tip from the presenters. Unless you want to portray a particular image, it is best not to look out of place. If you are in any doubt, ask the producer or researcher.

Breakfast television provides a good example of how styles differ from show to show. The BBC's *Breakfast News* is just that – a hard-news programme whose presenters dress in a smart, business-like fashion, as do the presenters on Sky's breakfast programme *Sunrise*. I would advise you to do the same. *GMTV* is less formal; guests and presenters sit on 'the sofa'. The male presenters wear suits, but the atmosphere is friendly and relaxed. Men may feel happy in a jacket rather than a suit, and women could wear something more casual. *The Big Breakfast* is aimed at a younger, trendier audience, so your most up-to-date clothes would be great!

As far as the cameras are concerned, avoid wearing narrow stripes or small checks as this can make the camera 'strobe' which is distracting for the viewer. Pastel-coloured shirts are more flattering for men, as white can drain the colour from a pallid face. Depending on the programme, I would advise a blue or grey suit with a bright tie for a formal interview. For a more casual show, possibly a favourite jacket (provided it is not hound's-tooth check) or sweater.

Women have a much wider choice of outfits, but this often makes it more difficult to decide what to wear. Judyth Halpin runs First Impressions, a company that advises on corporate image. 'Colour,' she says, 'is one of the first things we notice about a person, especially a woman, so it's important to get it right. If a colour causes someone to look tired or wan, it is more difficult to make a positive impact.' Extremes of colour are best avoided on television. Black can look funereal and some cameras do not like white as it tends to reflect the studio lights. Red can still cause a problem as it tends to 'bleed'. If you get a chance to watch the programme on which you are going to appear, look at the set. If it is very bright, then try to wear a colour that will contrast. If the set is fairly neutral (as is the case with most news or magazine programmes), than you can afford to wear stronger colours. Here are some very general outlines for different hair colours.

Blonde

Blue-greens are very flattering, as are soft yellows, coral or salmon pink. Avoid very dark colours, as they can create a strong contrast and distract attention.

Brunette or Black

Strong colours are best, such as olive green, royal blue, purple, bright-yellow or navy. If the skin is very pale, try turquoise, emerald green or deep pinks.

Golden, Red or Auburn
Golden-browns, olives, rusts and camels will work for you. Avoid darker shades of grey or navy.

Mid- or Light-brown
Brighter, lighter shades are preferable. If the skin is pale, pinks, blue-greens, lilac and yellows are best. Darker-skinned women should try rusts, moss green, medium blue or lemon yellow.

Grey
Blues, pinks, burgundy, plum and soft turquoise are good. Steer clear of very bright colours as they can be overpowering.

Colour Messages

As I am no expert on the complicated subject of colour analysis, I will not go into detail. You should be aware, however, that certain colours send out certain signals. Red is a strong, assertive colour, whereas blue is more neutral, but still business-like (make sure you do not melt into the background, though, as many studio 'cycs' or backdrops are blue). I know some television directors who dislike green for white skin as it tends to make them look sickly. Yellow is a good colour for dark or black skin. If in doubt – ask!

Choosing Flattering Styles

For the majority of television interviews the shot is mainly of the head and shoulders as people are usually sitting; even a full-length shot becomes a close-up when the interviewee starts to talk. A well-cut, plain jacket will always be appropriate, especially if you are delivering a strong message. Physical shape obviously makes a difference. If you have a short neck, choose open necklines or boat- or V-necked styles. For you, shorter hairstyles are preferable to long ones. If your neck is long, a scarf, choker or necklace will enhance the line, so will a stand-up collar. Shoulder length hair is the most flattering.

The length of clothes is important too. If you are short-waisted, longer jackets with skirts or trousers, narrow belts and drop-waisted dresses fit well. If you are long-waisted, choose cropped or bolero jackets, broad belts and empire-line dresses. If you have broad shoulders, do not wear shoulder pads or boat necklines; on the other hand, shoulder pads and V necks help to disguise a big bust. Tall women look good in three-quarter-length or long jackets, especially with long skirts; small women look better in short or cropped jackets with trousers, as it gives the feeling of longer legs. When sitting, short skirts are fine, but beware of showing too much leg – unless of course you want to!

Flashing jewellery and large earrings can send out the wrong messages and can also be a distraction. Long neck-laces should be avoided as they tend to interfere with a clip-on microphone; while on radio, big bracelets are a problem if they bang the microphone or table. Generally, anything that jangles is bad news.

Glasses

If you normally wear glasses, leave them on during the interview. Half-moon glasses are the only exception to this rule as they can totally obscure the eyes at certain angles. It is important that the viewers as well as the interviewer can see your eyes, so use an alternative pair if you have one. If you appear regularly on television, non-reflective lenses are a good investment. Tinted or 'reactalite' lenses are a bad idea as they can obscure the eyes completely and make you look like a member of the Mob!

Make-up

Although most television stations have make-up facilities, it is not always the case. If you are interviewed on your premises, then a make-up artist may not be in the crew. For men, a dusting of translucent powder is advisable, so if you know a camera crew is about to descend on you, pay a visit to a make-up counter!

Most women know how to apply some make-up. Wear what you would normally wear, but apply a bit more powder over your foundation or base. Press in the powder gently with a puff – do not be alarmed if it looks rather heavy, as it will soon be absorbed and it will last much longer. Blusher should be used in moderation; dusty pinks, salmon or terracotta tints are best. Try not to use too much dark eyeshadow; soft shades of brown used with a natural or pinky highlighter work well. If you use an eyeliner, define only about a third of the upper and lower lids with a colour such as plum, navy or dark-green, rather than black, before applying mascara.

Lipstick is important as it should enhance, but not draw attention to, the mouth as well as complementing your clothes. A lip pencil helps to define the lips and should be a similar, but slightly darker, shade than the lipstick. Powdering the lips first helps prevent lipstick from being absorbed too quickly. If there is a long gap between the time when you have done your make-up and the time you start the interview, be sure to recheck hair, powder and lips.

How to Sit

It is important to sit properly with your bottom at the back of the seat. This prevents you from slouching and also leaves your airways clear so that an attack of nerves will not make you breathless. A good tip is to sit on the tail of your jacket so that the collar does not ride up. Crossing and uncrossing legs can distract both interviewer and viewers; this is true for men and women. If you are a man and like to sit with crossed legs, make sure there is not a huge hairy gap between your socks and the hem of your trousers – a pair of long socks is essential. Women should carry a spare pair of tights as a ladder snaking up a leg will almost certainly take the viewers' minds off what you are saying!

Where to Look

The first question I am usually asked is 'Where do I look – at you or the camera?' You look at the interviewer, just as you would look at anyone with whom you are having a conversation.

'OVER-REHEARSING'

Some less-experienced interviewers tend to over-rehearse. This is especially true of some celebrities who stand in when the usual presenter is on holiday. This can be dangerous. Try not to let them take you through the subject too thoroughly, because if you have covered all the ground, you will find it very difficult to be as spontaneous when it comes to the 'take'.

EDITING

The reporter is often looking for a good soundbite or a point that has been well made. They have to cut out the waffle, or the time spent settling down at the beginning of the interview. If a statement is made in a rambling, roundabout way, then the journalist may decide to cover it with a 'voice-over' instead. Most producers would agree that good editing is hard to achieve, as the important elements can be a nuance, an aside or an emotion. Good editing should satisfy the interviewee as well as the programme makers. Many people are worried about their interview being edited to alter the meaning of what they have said. Although this is quite easy in technical terms, there are very strict guidelines that have to be followed. Nonetheless, I have known reporters who have 're-voiced' different questions back at the studio to give them the angle they were looking for, but this practice is severely frowned on.

There was a case a few years ago of a distinguished surgeon from Liverpool who appeared in a television documentary about the ethics of transplants. He was edited to make it appear that he and his team were not too careful in ensuring people were quite dead before they whipped their kidneys out. The surgeon was absolutely furious and threatened to sue the director, the producer and even the programme controller. He eventually forced them to broadcast a retraction, but it took two years before the levels of kidney donors in the Northwest reached the levels they had been before the programme was transmitted. This kind of instance is, however, less likely to happen today. The BBC investigates every complaint and the Independent Broadcasting Authority comes down heavily on any television company that transgresses the rules of what they deem honest and fair. As an interviewee you have the right to be treated fairly and have your interview edited fairly so that it is a proper representation of what you have said.

Some producers find it useful to conduct an interview in which more aspects of the topic are covered than are needed. Three areas may be discussed, but only one may be relevant, so the interview will be edited for that one point. Politicians and industrialists in the public eye know that if they speak clearly and to the point, and answer questions in a straightforward way, it will make the editing that much easier. People who waffle are the ones that cause the problems, both for themselves and the editors.

One way to guard against the problems of editing is to offer to do the piece live; another is to take a tape recorder with you, so that you also have a record of what was said. Do not be too disheartened if your interview only receives thirty seconds of air-time instead of the anticipated three minutes; there could be all manner of reasons for this. The usual one is that news has come in, reducing the pre-recorded items or sometimes (if it is a big story) losing them altogether. If, however, they have voiced over much of what you have said, then you were not getting to, and sticking to, the point!

When You Say 'Yes'!

If you have said 'yes' and agreed to be interviewed, it is a good idea to try and encapsulate your message in one sentence and start from there. Apart from providing the sound-bite most journalists are looking for, it has the added advantage of helping you to get your message in focus. Some journalists actually ask the question: 'If you have one message (in five seconds please!) what would it be?'; or 'How do you see the future?' Having the answers to these two questions will enable you to end the interview on a positive note – sometimes a word will do. When a past chairman of British Nuclear Fuels Limited was asked (with ten seconds to go) how the company would tackle the immensely complicated task of converting nuclear waste into glass, he answered: 'Safely'.

In my view, it is to your advantage to get to know and co-operate with the media, and the better you get to know them the harder they will find it to set you up. At the end of the day, though, only you can make the final decision – Yes or No.

CONCLUSION

Be as honest as you can without compromising yourself or your organization. Most journalists appreciate the time and trouble people take to accommodate them and will react accordingly. If you are very nervous, say so. It is in the presenter's interest to have you as relaxed and happy as possible. Above all, when the interview is about to start, remember that you are not the only person whose heart is thumping, mouth is dry or mind is on the verge of going blank! Television is an exhilarating medium in which to work, and everybody connected with it feels their nerves tingling as the cameras roll, the microphones are faded up and the studio goes live.

chapter three

THE KEY TO SUCCESS

Preparation is the key to confidence, and confidence is the key to success. The better prepared you are the more you will enjoy the interview experience.

TARGETING YOUR AUDIENCE

Preparation starts with thinking about the audience. The greatest incentives to get anyone to listen to us are fear, greed, topicality and sex! God forbid that you should try and frighten your audience out of its wits, but if you can put yourself between the public and adversity, you will gain their attention. Similarly, if you can construct your argument to help save your viewers, readers or listeners hassle, time or money, you will gain and keep their undivided attention.

Human nature is such that we are all basically selfish, and unless something has relevance for us we are not really interested. If there is news of a motorway accident, the first thought that goes through our minds is 'Do I know anyone who was in the area?' If, on the other hand, we hear of a massive premium-bond win, we will dig out our bonds to see if Ernie has come up trumps for us at last.

The subject on which you are going to be interviewed

will probably not fascinate every single member of your audience. That would be impossible. The best you can do is to play on human nature, and try and make what you say relate to as wide a range of people as possible. Take the use of fear, with the police as an example. Say they have been criticized for spending too much of their time and resources in catching and fining speeding motorists rather than preventing and detecting more serious crime. The positive response would be: 'Speeding is an extremely serious offence and can cause untold heartache and unhappiness. I hope you will never have to be the one to tell a mother that her son has been knocked down and seriously hurt by a driver doing fifty in a thirty-mile limit; or worse still, extricate five bodies from a car involved in a high-speed crash. Every time you see a police radar trap, you should be thankful that we are doing out best to protect you and your family.' The negative response would be something like: 'We only have a limited number of resources and we have to deploy these as best we can. Speeding may not seem a serious offence to you, but it is breaking the law like any other crime and it's our duty to try and put a stop to it.'

A picture paints a thousand words, and if you can use examples or analogies that will help your audience identify with your message, so much the better. For instance 'the size of the average house' rather than 'so many square metres', or 'as heavy as a bag of sugar' instead of 'two point two kilos'. Research has shown that we view television and listen to the radio with the concentration and intelligence of an average twelve-year-old. This is not because we are all stupid, but because we are not giving it our full attention. Bear this in mind, and keep your language simple. Obscure words or phrases will alienate your audience. During the average interview, which lasts for two to three minutes, it is wise to aim to leave no more than three points of fact or philosophy in the viewer or listener's mind. It is remarkable how many people fail to get their points across; they either say that they were not expecting the questions that were asked, or that the interviewer did not give them the chance. You have to make your own chances!

LISTENING

One of the key skills when being interviewed is listening. Although it sounds obvious, it is surprising how many people (usually through nerves) think they have heard the question and rush into the answer. Listen not only to the question, but to the question behind the question. Michael Barratt, who has seen all sorts of interviewees over the years, both before and after he presented BBC's *Nationwide*, says 'The art of talking is the art of listening. It's so easy to half hear the question, thinking that it is what you were expecting, on the topic you were expecting. You answer it, but you're not answering it. The effect on the viewers is that the question has been dodged, which raises doubts about your credibility.' Credibility is what you must aim for, both with the viewers and the journalists.

HELPFUL PHRASES

To help you get your message across, there are some useful phrases such as:

- 'That's a very important point, but to put it in context we have to go back ...'
- 'It's essential to realize that ...'
- 'To understand the situation properly ...'

Avoid the politician's old trick: saying 'That's a very interesting question' and then answering something completely different. The audience is not made up of idiots, and will know whether you have answered the question or not. If you do not know the answer then say so. It is far better to be honest than to waffle. If you are asked a question to which you should know the answer but do not, then say that you will do your best to find out.

The areas to be covered should have been mapped out before the interview. If you are asked questions which stray outside that area, do not answer them. Tell the reporter politely that you would be happy to come on another programme to discuss the topic at another time (if that is the case), and guide him or her back to the subject on which you agreed to be interviewed. Using phrases like these will help:

- 'If we can get back to ... which is what I thought we were here to discuss', or
- 'I think your viewers would be more interested to know why ...'

USING NOTES

On television or radio it is better not to use notes. If you are worried about forgetting significant facts, write them on a card which you can carry in your pocket to check before going into the studio. If you do need to check them, hold them up so that the viewers can see what you are doing. Avoid furtive glances – they make you look shifty. Do not forget that you have been asked to contribute to the programme because you know what you are talking about and are an expert in your field, so if you are constantly glancing down at your notes, again, it undermines your credibility. Files, clipboards or large pieces of paper can flutter, or be dropped by fingers trembling with nerves, which is bad news on either radio or television.

PREPARING FOR THE WORST

If you are worried about the accuracy of an interview (*see page 55*), it is a good idea to tape it. Tell the journalist what you are going to do, saying something like: 'I'm sure this won't happen today, but I was misquoted rather badly the last time I was interviewed, so do you mind if I record this?' Try not to appear paranoid as this could colour the piece they write about you (if it is a press interview). If you feel you might not be given a fair deal and the issue is really contentious, take someone along with you. Some press reporters will record the interview if their shorthand is a bit rusty, but beware of being caught off guard – if they turn the tape off or put their notebook down and continue to chat away, do not assume the interview has ended. In most cases, however, if you can relax enough to enjoy listening to and answering the questions, you will give a much better interview.

Some people believe that a journalist's main skill is to be able to write a readable piece or to conduct an incisive interview regardless of whether he or she really knows anything about the subject. That is indeed true, but today's journalists tend to specialize and have more than a good working knowledge of their subject; if you are in any doubt, you can test the depth of their knowledge with a few relevant questions. Nevertheless, it is always as well to make sure they have understood the basic facts, ensuring you are on the same wavelength.

The two other main areas for preparation are the voice and the body. These are covered in detail in Chapter 4.

MAKING A POSITIVE IMPACT

To help create that all-important positive impact when making a public appearance of any kind, remember 'the three Es':

- energy
- enthusiasm
- enjoyment

Energy

The energy must come from within. However earth-shattering your message may be, it will have little or no impact if it is delivered in a dull, boring, lacklustre way. The energy in your voice and body must shine through, showing that you are willing and able to talk on your topic in a confident and competent manner.

Enthusiasm

Enthusiasm is perhaps the most important 'E' of all. If you are not enthusiastic about your subject then why should your audience be? Think of the people who interest you. What is it that makes you tune in and listen to them? It is usually because they especially want to tell you about their particular subject.

This does not mean that you should get so enthusiastic that you become carried away and lose sight of your audience! The fact that you have interesting information should allow your natural enthusiasm to come across.

Enjoyment

Enjoyment comes from the fact that you have prepared. You have asked all the relevant questions and hopefully received the necessary answers; so now you can really begin to relax and enjoy the interview.

CONCLUSION

The secret of success lies in the preparation. When you are in the spotlight, you have to be able to deliver the goods. So regardless how rough you feel, notwithstanding the problems you may have at home or at work, your preparation will pull you through. If you have looked deeply into all likely areas of questioning, and are confident that you can answer them; if you have worked on your voice and body so that you can relax as much as possible, then you should come across to the viewers as an interesting expert in your field, rather than some granite-faced individual lacking any personality or presence.

It is equally important, however, to remember not to cross the line between confidence and arrogance, especially in a confrontational situation. Make yourself difficult to dislike and aim to retain public sympathy. You must win your arguments but never on a knock-out!

chapter four

THE BODY, THE MIND AND THE MOUTH

Within the first thirty seconds of meeting someone, we form eighty per cent of our opinion of them. A pretty horrendous thought! But if you analyse it, you will agree that it is probably true. In a job interview, for example, the moment the candidate walks through the door we make a snap decision; the same is true at parties – the first impression is the one that makes us want to get to know someone better (or not as the case may be!). Obviously, that decision is not final, and will often change; but on television or radio you have no time for a second chance. If you do not make a positive impact straightaway, the audience will vote by switching to another channel or turning off altogether. So how do you go about making that vital first impression?

COMMUNICATION

Communication is what life is all about, and yet many of us find it hard to get through to other people on a face-to-face level, never mind through the artificial and often prejudicial organs of the media. As with any situation, we cannot assume that people understand what we mean; we have to make sure that they see the story from our point of view. In a classic case of misinterpreted messages, British Rail put up a sign at level crossings: 'Don't cross the line while a train is approaching.' In parts of the north of England the word 'while' is used as 'until'! After a couple of near misses and numerous complaints, the wording was changed. In an interview, it is essential to make sure that you and the journalist are on the same wavelength. To interact successfully we have two main instruments of communication: the voice and the body.

THE VOICE

We all have a diverse vocal range, but most of us use only a fraction of it. Men are usually worse than women. I put it down to puberty – boys are not sure where their voices are going to end up, so they play safe and speak on one level. Women, on the other hand, can suddenly find that their voices are reduced to a series of squeaks when very nervous. In Chapter 10, I have included some vocal exercises to help improve breathing, voice production and diction.

It still surprises me that so many people who regularly speak in public have never really listened to or analysed their voices. How can you play an instrument if you do not know how it sounds? The voice is a wonderful instrument; it can inform, cajole, excite, anger, soothe – anything you want it to – if used properly. This is true not only on radio or television, but throughout everyday life, at home or at work. If you have young children, why not set a tape recorder running when reading them bedtime stories? Get to know what it feels like to use your upper and lower registers as you read the parts of different characters. Throw away your inhibitions! If you have a video camera, use it to record a presentation or talk. Get to know what you look like when you are sitting, standing, talking, laughing or listening. I cannot stress enough the importance of listening to your voice. You need to know whether there is a reasonable amount of expression in it, how fast you speak and the pitch of your voice; is it high or low? How loudly do you speak, and how clearly? Are you using the three Es (*see page 63*)?

'Ums' and 'Ers'

Sometimes I am accused of trying to make actors, or worse still, 'clones' out of men and women who appear on a public platform. This is absolutely untrue. Your presentation style must fit you like a second skin, be it for public speaking or media appearances. It is important, however, to know whether you preface your answers with irritating 'thinking time' – words like 'I mean', 'so', 'well', 'right', 'OK' – or the dreaded 'ums' and 'ers'. If you have an interview coming up, think of some likely questions, and get a partner or colleague to interview you. Record it and then play it back to see if you came across as you intended. Are you using the same phrases repeatedly, or expressions such as 'you know' and 'kind of'?

Accents

Regional accents do not matter (in fact they can be an advantage) but clear speech does. If people cannot hear what you say they will switch off mentally, if not physically. The speech exercises in Chapter 10 will help to you judge your diction, and improve it if necessary.

Vocal Exercises

One of the exercises we do when training radio and television newscasters is to ask them to read the words in a way that heralds the story. Take a simple phrase like 'A man from Preston ...' and assume that it prefaces three very different stories:

- A man from Preston was killed this afternoon in a hit-and-run accident. Police are appealing for witnesses.
- A man from Preston has won over two million pounds on the Pools today. It was the first time he had ever filled in a coupon.
- A man from Preston has been elected as chair of Lancashire's new opera company. He takes up the post in January.

Each of these sentences will be said with a different inflection. The first is obviously fairly sombre, with a downward inflection. The second is a happy story and is therefore delivered faster, with an upward inflection. The third is more balanced, as the news is neither bad nor good. The way we 'tee up' a story helps prepare our audience for what is to come. You can put this to the test by analysing the way in which newsreaders deliver the opening words of each story, and you will realize just how much they are signposting the mood of the bulletin. The more interesting and digestible you make your message, the more easily it will be assimilated.

It is Not Just What You Say ...

What you say is of major consequence, but analysts claim that audience reaction to what you are saying can be judged thus:

- 58 per cent by appearance
- 35 per cent by voice
- 7 per cent by content

Frightening, but a simple example demonstrates the truth of this claim. If somebody said 'I'm sorry' with a smile on her face, it is unlikely you would believe her; if, on the other hand, she said it with tears in her eyes, you probably would. It was claimed that approximately sixty per cent of people who voted for Ronald Reagan disagreed with his policies but thought he was a nice guy!

These examples highlight the power of the media, and the significance of the image you portray. Having said all that, the most important thing is to be yourself.

THE BODY

The Smile

If our body does not work in harmony with our voice the wrong signals can be transmitted, both consciously and sub-consciously. Even if you are in the studio to answer accusations on a sensitive issue it is important to smile when introduced. Obviously there are exceptional circumstances, but on the whole a smile does two things: it helps to break the barrier that exists between the camera lens, the television screen and the viewer; and it relaxes the muscles round the mouth that can make us look as if we are auditioning to be ventriloquists when paralysed by nerves!

Body Language

Some researchers estimate that as much as seventy per cent of what influences viewers watching a television interview comes from body language. It is essential, then, that we give the right signals. Positive body language comes from being relaxed and knowing your subject; it usually expresses our unconscious feelings and emotions and cannot be learnt. Nevertheless, there are certain mannerisms that should be avoided. A little knowledge can be a dangerous thing, and a viewer who has been on body-language courses or read books on the subject can sometimes see signs that are not there! I personally do not think we should get too hooked up on it because it can make us appear unnatural and get in the way of what we are saying. There are, however, a few exercises that can help to evaluate body language in ourselves, which we can then learn to apply to others.

Take a mental note of your own gestures and posture as your mood and feelings change in conversations or meetings. Asking yourself the following questions will help you build up a picture of your body-language vocabulary:

- Are you leaning forward or back?
- Are your legs apart or crossed?
- Is your brow furrowed when you concentrate?
- Do you listen with head on one side, or nod in agreement as you mentally concur with the speaker?
- Are your fists clenched or are your hands relaxed with the palms open?
- Are your arms folded across the body if you are sceptical or disagree with a point of view?
- Are you hiding any vulnerable areas, such as putting your hand over your genital region, if you feel unsure of yourself or your subject?

When watching interviews on television, turn the sound down for a few seconds and see if you have accurately read the mood before listening to the rest of the interview.

Negative Signals

Anxiety is an infectious emotion that manifests itself in several forms, the most evident being the wringing of hands, clenching of fists, running fingers through hair or rubbing the back of the neck. The latter two can also show frustration or exasperation. Playing with cuffs, rings, bracelets or ties shows a feeling of uncertainly that can also make you look less than confident.

Crossing and uncrossing the legs, foot tapping or 'walking' gestures are all subconsciously saying that you do not want to be there and cannot wait to get out of the studio. It is no good sounding and looking calm only from the waist up; good directors will ask for a wide shot if they feel that your body is contradicting your mouth. Make a note of the most negative signals (like putting a hand in front of the face or folding arms across the chest) and try to avoid them. I often fold my arms across my chest when I am cold, but I would make sure this did not happen during an interview no matter how icy the studio because it could be construed as a negative, defensive gesture. Likewise, be aware of your hands; drumming fingers play havoc with microphones and show a similar sense of shiftiness and unease. All these things send out negative signals. As I have mentioned before, it is essential that you come across as the warm, confident person that you are!

Reading a Journalist's Body Language

The Handshake

When you first meet a journalist or presenter, there are certain indications of stance and behaviour that can be very revealing. Take something as simple as the handshake. The person to offer the hand is generally the most assertive; if no hand is offered in return, then either that person has a contagious disease, or he is trying to put you down! The way the hand is offered is interesting. A dominant handshake is offered with the palm face down; a submissive handshake is when the palm faces up. The one you should be aiming for is to be on equal terms – arm outstretched with the hand horizontal, thumb facing upwards. The strength of the contact is also quite an indicator of character. I am always wary of people who offer me a 'wet fish' as I view it as a sign of indecisiveness.

Posture

There is a big difference between confidence and arrogance; over-confidence or superiority is often displayed by the way someone sits – hands clasped behind the head, leaning back in the chair with the legs outstretched and ankles crossed. A journalist adopting this position could well take some convincing! Someone who is sitting forward in the chair or leaning on a desk, perhaps forming a 'steeple' with the fingers, is much more likely to be listening impartially and with interest to what you have to say. Glasses often have a role to play. Some reporters gain thinking time by polishing their glasses or slowly and deliberately folding them to discomfit an interviewee before asking the next question. On radio or television, the journalist or presenter is responsible for the continuity of any interview, so do not be tempted to jump in and fill that gap.

Eye Contact

Eye contact is critical. You cannot read another person unless you can see into his or her eyes. Watch for shifts in eye contact, for the steady interrogating gaze, for the blank look that could mean the reporter has forgotten your name or the next question!

Warning Signals

There are certain signs that will tell us when a press journalist is getting bored during an interview, a yawn being the most obvious! Common signals of disinterest are a lowered head, lack of eye contact, fiddling with a pen, doodling or clasping the face with one or both hands.

The boredom is usually caused by the interviewee not getting to the point or trotting out the same old party line.

Alternatively, it could be that the journalist has already written the story and is just waiting for a gem from you to finish it off. An experienced reporter will sometimes fake boredom to encourage you to talk more on a particular topic, hoping you may drop your guard.

Timing Signals

A surreptitious glance at the clock from a radio presenter will tell you that time has passed and the interview will shortly come to an end. On television, the passage of time is more difficult to detect, but if the presenter shifts forward in the chair, starts nodding in agreement or breaking into your answers, read these as signs that time is running out and keep your replies short and to the point, as well as bringing in any remaining relevant issues.

Signs of Interest

If somebody is interested in what you are saying, he or she will usually look you in the eye, smile and nod encouragingly. If the listener's pupils enlarge, then this is a sign that you are getting on very well indeed! Again, you have to remember that being two-faced is one of the requirements that make a good journalist. If you are dealing with cynical people you have to be cynical too.

LEARNING TO RELAX

It is not easy to relax in a studio. The main reason for nervousness is audience reaction. The audience may be the viewers or listeners at home, a live audience in a studio or even the camera crew and technicians. Nobody likes to make a fool of themselves. The problems start as the body begins pumping adrenalin to produce the 'fight or flight' reaction needed when man was a hunter confronted by a sabre-toothed tiger. Since most presenters are not that grue-some, we do not need such strong stimulation!

Cary Cooper, Professor of Organisational Psychology at the Manchester School of Management, UMIST, has a few tips to help calm those nerves. As the pulse and breath-rate quicken we need to keep the adrenalin under control. The worst thing to do is sit still. Find out where the toilets are and pay the occasional visit if there is a long wait before you are on in the programme. Try to arrive early so that you can have a glance inside the studio and chat to the crew if they are not busy. If possible, have a word with the presenter before the programme. This may not always be feasible, but most presenters will do their best to put you at your ease, as will the other studio personnel. In Chapter 10, I have includ-ed some breathing and relaxation exercises to help ease the tension. These can be done in the privacy of your car when you reach the studios, or in the toilet if stress threatens to overwhelm you.

Do not Give the Game Away

By all means chat to the other contributors who may be waiting with you, but guard against discussing the inter-view, unless it is with the researcher who has been your con-tact, and even then do not say too much. You would be amazed how many people drop themselves in it with phras-es like: 'I hope they don't ask me about the plant in Wakefield – it's a real time-bomb!' Any researchers worth their salt would go straight to the presenter with the advice 'Ask him about Wakefield.'

Staying Power

Food plays a significant part in how we perform, as does drink. I think the general rule should be 'if in doubt leave alcohol out'. People often think it will help steady the nerves but forget that it can loosen the tongue. If you suffer from a dry mouth when nervous, then stick to water before the programme, as too much tea and coffee act as a diuretic. To keep my adrenalin coursing during long days of filming when there are still many 'takes' to do, my favourite director always whispers 'sparkle, sparkle, sparkle' just before the camera rolls! It is a good tip, because a sparkle is what you should aim for.

Edwina Curry MP has media experience on both sides of the camera. She stresses the importance of eating well and keeping fit. 'You can't think quickly if you're over-tired, so getting enough sleep should be high on the agenda. I also try to make sure that I am not hungry before an interview, as it can have an effect on energy levels.' Get to know your own body. Does your tummy rumble at eleven in the morning? If so, make sure you munch a biscuit or a slice of bread before going to the studio. Does your blood sugar ebb in the afternoon? Sucking a glucose sweet or eating a banana can help as a quick pick-me-up.

A light meal is preferable before an interview, as you do not want to feel drowsy from too much food. The studios usually provide sandwiches or a cold buffet as well as hot and cold drinks. The *Today* programme supplies toast, buns and croissants for the early risers, but regional programmes do not usually have the budget for much more than coffee and biscuits! However, there is always the canteen. If you are in the studios for some time, perhaps contributing to several radio programmes in the space of a couple of hours, then liquid is vital to keep both the spirits and the voice level high. If you are not offered a drink then do ask for one.

BUILDING CONFIDENCE

What worries people most when they stand up to speak in public or take part in a radio or television programme is the fear that they will forget everything – even their own name. I cannot stress it often enough – preparation is the key to confidence. You can help build confidence by making a list of your:

- strengths
- talents
- skills
- achievements

CONCLUSION

It is important to realize just what we are capable of. We must also recognize our weak points so that we can strengthen them. Think positive thoughts! A good quotation to remember when the spirits are flagging comes from Winston Churchill: 'A pessimist always sees a calamity in every opportunity. An optimist sees an opportunity in every calamity.' Make sure you are prepared to make the most of your media opportunity.

chapter five

THE PROGRAMMES

RADIO

There are basically two types of radio show that you are likely to take part in – all speech or speech and music. If you are asked in 'for a chat' during a music-based programme the duration depends on how long the DJ talks between records. The questions are usually more general, to appeal to a wide lay audience, and there is usually less time to meet the presenter beforehand. You may think that what you wear on radio does not matter, but it definitely has a bearing on how you sound. It is as well not to wear anything that will rustle too much, and I advise clothes that are comfortable. If you always wear a suit for work and you are being interviewed on a work-related subject, then wear a suit. Apart from making you feel right, it will give you credibility as far as the interviewer is concerned.

The Phone-in

The phone-in can give you a longer stint on the air than the average interview. It also gives you added credibility, portraying you as an expert in your field. Doctors, solicitors, policemen, vets and politicians make regular contributions to both national and local phone-in programmes, as do culinary, dietary, DIY and gardening gurus. It will do you or your practice no harm at all to be heard regularly giving good advice, and it could be advisable to offer your services to these sort of programmes if you have the time. People often worry that they will not know the answers to half the questions; if there are problems, tell the caller that the answer is too long, or too complicated, to explain over the air, take the name and address and send the information.

National Radio News Programmes

In a fast-moving news programme a sharp brain is needed by the interviewer no matter what time of day or night it is. John Humphries has been a presenter on *Today* for the past seven or eight years, and he has got his early-morning routine down to a fine art. His alarm goes off at 4 a.m., and he is out of the shower and into the taxi in about seven minutes, and then out of the taxi and into the BBC in Portland Place in another eight minutes – so from bed to the Beeb in about a quarter of an hour! He then has a bowl of home-made muesli, flips through the papers, reads a few scripts and writes the introductions to his interviews. 'In theory I try to look at who I'm going to be interviewing, though in practice the brain doesn't seem to be terribly co-operative at that time in the morning, and I find I can't really think about the interviews until I'm about to do them. My brain seems to be saying "Come on, I don't really want to be doing this." It would rather be reading a bit of gossip in the newspapers!'

The *Today* programme has teams of researchers who work twelve-hour shifts, so any news that comes in from anywhere in the world is picked up and sifted. The amount of information the presenter is given about the interviewees depends on when it is available. Most of the interviews are set up the night before, unless a mega story breaks. John usually has no idea who is coming on the programme until he arrives in the building, unless it is the prime minister or a member of the royal family. Most of the time the interviewee dictates where the discussion will go. 'An interview on a programme like *Today* should be a conversation. It shouldn't be a rigorously rehearsed set piece intellectual exercise. What we seek to achieve is to give the audience something easy to listen to. Stimulating and informative, but easy to listen to.'

As we talked in the studio during 'YIP' ('Yesterday in Parliament'), the engineering 'cubicle' on the other side of the glass was full of people – technicians, researchers and the editor of the day. While Sue McGregor was doing her last interview of the morning, I noticed John writing furiously. The editor had told him through his headphones that there was a telephone interview coming up. This happens quite often on a programme like *Today*, where news is coming in all the time. One such occasion was an interview with the prime minister of India. There was no time for a briefing before he came on the phone, so with nothing to go on, John opened the interview with the question: 'Tell me prime minister, how serious is the situation?', and went on from there!

Not everyone works in the same way. Sue McGregor likes to have more information, and works out a line of questioning beforehand. In the event of a major interview, the editor will also have his own thoughts of how he sees the story, and discussions take place either before the programme starts, or when they are actually on the air. This is true of most news programmes. News is by definition immediate, so if a story breaks that could involve you, be ready for a call. You may be given as little as half an hour's warning to do a 'down the line' radio interview, so make sure you have enough time to get your thoughts and facts in order.

James Naughtie is now a presenter on *Today*, but he told me about his experiences when he anchored *The World At*

One. A typical day for that team starts at 7.30 a.m., when they will arrive at Broadcasting House in Portland Place and listen to *Today* and watch *Breakfast News*. By 8.30 a.m. they will have digested the papers and will work out the kind of programme they want to put on the air. They give their listeners what they feel they want to know as well as trying to push stories on and add to what has been said already. The journalistic edge of the programme is to say something new and significant. One of the ways in which they judge their success is the number of items that are picked up by other programmes and newspapers. They insist this does not mean that the media is incestuous, and just competing with other programmes or trying to score points. James admits, however, that there is an element of competition with other radio programmes, just as there is between, say, *The Guardian* and *The Independent*. *The World At One* wants to get the interview another programme failed to get, but James feels that is a good thing and keeps journalists sharp. 'We can't be dogmatic about people's taste, but we must make the best judgement we can about what we feel is important.'

In some cases that judgement is relatively easy. If the prime minister is making a statement on Sinn Fein, for example, it is obviously more important than the speech being made by Mr X at the CBI Conference. Editors and journalists also have to decide what is going to interest people, and these are things that are argued round the table during editorial meetings. On the subject of rail privatization, for instance, the questions people want asked are whether railcards are going to survive, if services will be cut and whether fares will go up. The questions are usually direct:

- Why did you say that?
- What does it mean?
- What is going to happen next?

There can be very strong feelings from different journalists about what interests people, and a lot of research is done to find out what people think. One of the biggest elements of BBC bureaucracy is collating audience reaction. Huge reams of paper come into news and current affairs offices every day, telling them how many people have called up about this or that item and what they have said. Letters are taken extremely seriously. Trends are analysed, as there is no point in making a programme nobody wants to listen to.

James Naughtie's preparation varies enormously. On an average morning for *The World At One* it was quite common to record eight or nine interviews with very little time between them in the two hours before the programme went on air. This sort of interview is usually fairly straightforward: the two-minute interview with the industrialist, the two-minute interview with the economist and the three-minute interview with the minister. If it is a prime ministerial interview, or if James is interviewing a government minister on a big policy document that is about to come out, it would involve a couple of afternoons sitting with colleagues working out lines of inquiry, and a lot of time reading cuttings. 'When you're trying to get something out of somebody, or if it's a policy issue and somebody has to be nailed to the wall because they're in the centre of some controversy, it requires a lot of thought. What you're trying to do is approach it the right way. This is partly so that you can demonstrate to the listener that you are asking the questions that they want to hear asked, and partly because there is also a certain amount of tactics involved, as you know there are things people don't want to say.'

Radio 5 Live provides a mixture of news, human-interest features and sport, and is aiming at a younger audience than Radio 4. The main reason for its birth was to enable the BBC to cover momentous events as they unfold. If the prime minister resigned there would be newsflashes on all networks, but as far as the BBC is concerned, 5 Live would stay with the story, so that anyone wanting an update could tune in twenty-four hours a day for the latest information. Their harder news programmes, as with other BBC networks, fill the breakfast, lunchtime and drive-time slots. They take as many live interviews as possible, and an interviewee, according to the editor of news programmes, will be treated with 'courtesy, kindness and thought'. The items and interviews throughout the day cover the widest range of topics, from opera to pay disputes, medical matters and a book review in the space of half an hour. The output is amazingly diverse and fast-moving.

Radio 5 Live is about news, so their main priority is to get people into the studio as fast as possible. As they like to keep the sound quality high, they may ask you to go to your nearest BBC studio to do a 'down the line' if you live outside London. If that is inconvenient, however, or there is not time, they would be happy to interview you over the phone. They are very keen to hear from anyone who has something interesting to say, and there is a central planning desk that sifts information before passing it on to the different programmes. Some programmes plan ahead, and may be in touch a couple of days before the interview, while others give very little notice. News comes in from various sources, including the national and regional papers, the wires and the BBC's General News Service (GNS).

Typical National Radio Daytime Programmes

There are programmes on the air all day, all over the country, and it would be impossible to mention them all in a book of this size. Suffice it to say, that the output of the vast majority of Independent Local Radio (ILR) stations is music, so you are most likely to be interviewed by the BBC or a national independent station such as Classic FM. Radio 4 and 5 Live are speech-based, while Radio 2 and Classic FM transmit music and some speech. Radios 1 and 3 carry mostly music, with some celebrity interviews and, in Radio 3's case, arts programmes.

The *Jimmy Young* programme on Radio 2 attracts a large number of loyal listeners. There are set strands on the programme and the producer, John Gurnett, knows what works after eighteen years on the show. As well as music, it carries a mixture of news, current affairs and information; and such is the calibre of the show that they have no trouble in persuading even the prime minister to come and be interviewed. John looks for 'a definite point of view' in the interviewees chosen for the programme, as well as someone who is lively and articulate.

John Dunn has two main guests on his Radio 2 show, apart from phone-ins and telephone interviews. John always researches and prepares thoroughly for everyone who comes on his programme, unlike some of his interviewees. 'I do beseech anyone trying to promote a book to re-read it. The time between the book's publication and when the author last looked at it can be quite considerable, and it's embarrassing if I seem to know their book better than they do!'

Woman's Hour on Radio 4 is a well-respected, well-established programme that covers any topic relevant to women. Anne Reevell, Senior Producer Radio Features, says, 'We are always on the lookout for material, and are glad to hear from people with good, interesting ideas or stories.' The items vary in length and some of the features take weeks to research. Interviewees are always well briefed, but Anne warns, 'If you're taking part in a discussion involving two or three people, it is essential to find out what the introduction is, and where you are supposed to stand on the issue.'

The content of *The Magazine* on 5 Live is decided only the afternoon before the following morning's programme, and interviewees may get no more than a few minutes' warning. For most of the interviews, they will be given a brief outline of what is wanted, but not the questions. The interviews are usually around two or three minutes long, unless it is a discussion, where the slot might be five or six minutes.

Radio Documentaries

Radio 4 puts out most documentaries at present. They cover all sorts of subjects and attract a dedicated team of broadcast journalists and producers. Felicity Goody spent two years working on *File On Four*, and it was not unusual for her to spend twelve to eighteen hours a day researching the items. She talked to huge numbers of people, and read volumes, digging deep into the background of any subject that was put under her microscope. If a 'radio doc' gets in touch, make sure you obtain as much information as you can, so that you can determine the angle they are looking for. Programmes like *Science Now*, *Law In Action* and *The Food Programme* are not documentaries in the same sense. Although they employ journalists to investigate particular subjects, they are not usually mounting an 'exposé'.

Local Radio

News

Into the newsrooms come stories from various different sources. Many are picked up in the local or national papers. When producers from radio and television ring to check the substance of a story, however, they quite often find it has been blown up out of all proportion. Other material comes from news agencies or the BBC's GNS, as well as being phoned through by stringers. There are also the mountains of press releases that land on the editor's desk in both national and local newsrooms.

Local radio wants local news. They do not have the resources to follow national stories even if that was their brief, so if you talk to local reporters about an idea or a story it must have a local angle. You will either be asked into the studio or a reporter will come to you. If you happen to be outside the area, the BBC will ask you to go to your nearest studio so that the sound quality of the interview will match the rest of the programme; failing this, they will talk to you over the phone.

If it seems that this section is giving too much emphasis to the BBC, it is because the majority of radio programmes to which you will be asked to contribute will be transmitted by the Beeb. ILR carries news on the hour and most independent stations play music ninety per cent of the time. The established independent stations, such as Capital Radio in London, have reduced their speech output over the years. They used to have various slots that they now leave to newer, more specialized stations or the BBC. Capital caters for a younger audience with features about music, work, health and sport. In their evening half-hour news magazine *The Way It Is*, the emphasis is on entertainment and is pitched at the same level as the tabloid press. They react to news events but do not rely purely on the papers for their ideas. The research time is very short, and average feature packages last from three to five minutes and will contain several interviews; ideally what they are looking for is the thirty-second soundbite.

Piccadilly Radio in Manchester is typical of most ILR stations. They have news interviews live, or pre-recorded, depending on the available studio time. On the whole, ILR caters for the under-forties, and the news is delivered in a sharp, snappy style. When a big story breaks, however, all available journalists will be sent out to cover the topic as thoroughly as possible from every angle, to give it as long a shelf life as possible.

Daytime Shows

On music-based daytime shows on local radio, the presenters are not usually journalists. As their expertise is in the music industry, they may not know too much about you or your topic. It is always as well to ask them how familiar they are with the subject so that you can fill in details that may be missing. A typical instance happened to Jo Wheeler, a presenter on Radio Lincolnshire. The usual presenter for that show was ill and Jo rushed in at the last minute to take over the programme, which included a large amount of sport. Football is not her subject, but there was no time to brief her about the gritty interview that was about to take place with the manager of the local team, so she was just handed a list of questions. When the manager came into the studio she had to tell him that she had no real knowledge of football, and asked him not to make a fool of her by using terms she would not understand. Sensibly, he was not tempted to show off, because although he may have had the upper hand on that occasion, you can bet your bottom dollar life could have been made difficult the next time he wanted publicity for his club!

The emphasis for most local radio daytime shows tends to be on entertainment, and journalists and presenters want you to provide interesting information for their listeners. They are not out to crucify you; they just want to hear your story. There are exceptions to every rule, however! Ed Doolan presents an afternoon show on Radio WM in Birmingham. He has a reputation for being tough and keeps his listeners riveted with his lively and sometimes aggressive interviews. 'There's nothing I enjoy more than confronting politicians who have something to hide, or won't come to the point. But I never really lose my temper on the air; it's always a controlled loss. However, I do leave the studio overjoyed when I've managed to put the boot in with a question they weren't expecting!' Ed also writes a column in the *Birmingham Evening Mail*. Some would say he sails pretty close to the wind as far as the libel laws are concerned, but he has never been sued because he constantly monitors his interviews and always prefaces his most damning remarks with phrases like: 'It has been said', 'I believe that', 'It has been alleged' or 'One could be forgiven for thinking'. He can turn quite ugly when people decline to comment. If a politician or councillor refuses to come on the programme to answer what he feels are his listeners' legitimate concerns, he will mention the fact as often as he can, for as long as he can. It is as well to remember that journalists have the power to keep a story running simply by making reference to the specific incident every time a name or an organization is mentioned. Local radio thrives on characters like Ed Doolan because they make interesting listening, are influential and have a large local following that should not be underestimated.

Sometimes it can be unnerving to be shown into a studio where you are confronted by a presenter who is busy playing records and does not even look up to acknowledge your entrance! Unfortunately, as in every profession, although some people start to believe their own publicity and become rather arrogant, most are not usually deliberately rude. They do have their hands full playing in various jingles and commercials, or picking out the next compact disc. Sit down and wait for them to speak to you. Always be as quiet as possible because you can never be sure when the microphone will be faded up. As some DJs are given very little information before an interview, start by asking them what the opening question is going to be, as that will give an indication of how much they know about you and your subject. These interviews are normally short in length, probably three or four minutes, and they are sometimes interspersed with music.

NATIONAL RADIO AND TELEVISION NEWS

The national news carries reports which are just that – of national importance. That does not mean they will not carry local stories, but when they do the items must have a nation-wide appeal. For instance, a series of fires that destroyed several schools in Stockport, Greater Manchester, made the headlines on the national news that day, and prominent spots the same night on the BBC's *Nine O'clock News*, ITV's *News At Ten* and *Sky News*. It was carried by the local media in the Northwest for three or four days, with in-depth reports on the causes and consequences. Any 'big' story will be made to run as long as it can, with new angles being sought to give the story as much staying power as possible. So where you may be interviewed for only a couple of min-utes, or edited down to a thirty-second soundbite for a national bulletin, another interview for the local programme will probably take longer and go into greater detail.

TYPICAL TELEVISION PROGRAMMES

Breakfast Time

When he presented BBC's *Breakfast News*, Nicholas Witchell's schedule was pretty hectic. He got to the studios at 3.30 a.m., and would leave after the programme at about 9.30 a.m. He would later return to Television Centre at 5.30 p.m., watch the *Six O'Clock News* and go into a planning meeting for the following morning's programme, which would last until around 7.15 p.m. He then went home to grab some sleep before getting up again just before 3 a.m. It is a cruel pace!

The items to be included in *Breakfast News* are largely

decided the night before, and the presenter does not normally have the chance to meet the interviewees before the programme. Nick used to prepare his interviews when he got to the studios in the morning. He would normally write down six or seven questions which would broadly cover the topics that he felt needed to be addressed. These would not necessarily all be used, and they would not inhibit him from following other topics that might emerge during the course of the interview. 'Obviously, as we were on the air for two hours, there were many occasions when a story broke during the programme, so I would have a few minutes or even a few seconds to put together an interview. But because it's a news programme, the questions will always be obvious. I wasn't doing a forty-minute, in-depth interview, just three or possibly five minutes.'

Eamon Holmes presents GMTV's breakfast programme. He sees the fundamental difference between their programme and *Breakfast News* or Sky's *Sunrise* as being the emphasis on entertainment. Like all commercial stations, GMTV needs to attract viewers, and they will tackle subjects that the others will not. Take the case of an interview with a nineteen-year-old boy who had killed a man when he tried to stop him stealing his car. The youth was convicted of manslaughter, much to the outrage of public opinion. GMTV's interview was in questionable taste, but the ratings went up and they had more publicity that week than they had done for months. It is easy to forget that programmes need promoting as much as people or events. Commercial television in this country looks set to follow the American lead, becoming more voyeuristic and sensational in order to pick up the most viewers. It is like the tabloid press – if we did not watch it, they would not show it! An interview on *GMTV* would cover the human angle of a story rather than the intellectual.

Eamon has worked as a journalist for many years, and he

thinks it is important to know your interviewer's background. Although he now works in what could broadly be
called light entertainment, as a journalist the fundamental
questions 'what, why, where, when and how' are always in
the forefront of his mind. Someone like Oprah Winfrey, who
was originally an actress, will also ask these questions, but
she will have the human angle very much to the fore; 'Does
it still haunt you? Can you ever forget the experience?'

Daytime

A daytime programme is likely to have a larger female following, but the audience is also made up of shift-workers,
pensioners, students and the unemployed. The pace is slower than at other times of the day because people have more
time to sit down and watch the television. *Kilroy* is a daily,
morning programme that tackles social issues of all kinds.
The studio audience is drawn from viewers who have an
axe to grind about a particular subject. Robert Kilroy-Silk's
objective is to produce 'informative entertainment' and,
when necessary, 'make those in authority accountable'.
Politicians or 'those in authority' are usually hugely out-
numbered. Despite what can be a difficult experience, the
programme has no trouble in attracting contributors; indeed
even MPs ring up with ideas for future topics.

The participants on *Kilroy* are given some information
about the structure of that day's subject and where they fit
in. Kilroy-Silk has been accused of stacking the odds against
the 'official'. He denies this, but advises them to stay out of
the kitchen if they cannot stand the heat. You have to ask
yourself what kind of temperatures you can stand, when
thinking of appearing on this type of audience-participation
programme.

Granada Television's *This Morning* has been winning the
morning ratings battle for the last few years. It includes top-

ics that appeal to a wide audience, although it is aimed mainly at women. There are production teams who are responsible for the programme on different days, and a number of the features or strands are produced by independent companies who face tough competition to win commissions. The programme moves very quickly, with items on cookery, fashion, antiques, interior design and more serious social issues like child abuse and divorce. The presenters are extremely professional and helpful. The studio is a converted warehouse at the Albert Dock on the waterfront in Liverpool, and is situated some way from the production offices and make-up room. In fact, it is the only studio I have ever worked in where you have to go outside again once you are made-up! I had a silly experience the last time I was on the programme. Liverpool is always windy (and cold) so I went to the studios in leggings, carrying the skirt I was intending to wear. By the time I got into make-up, the skirt had disappeared. It had actually been blown off the hanger as I carried it under my arm. I could not believe it, but the make-up artist just laughed and said 'You can kiss goodbye to that I'm afraid; it'll be halfway down the Mersey by now.' And it was!

Regional Programmes

The regional evening programme is the one you are most likely to appear on as far as television is concerned. These vary from area to area, especially on ITV, but the BBC's output is more uniform with a harder news slant. Again, the make-up of the audience is critical here. The age range is likely to be from nine to ninety, so you have to appeal to a general audience.

Is there a great difference between local and national television journalists? Philip Hayton anchors BBC's *Northwest Tonight* from Manchester. Before that he was a foreign correspondent for the BBC as well as presenting the national news bulletins at six and nine o'clock. He sees little difference in the way that regional BBC programmes and the national news handle a story as far as the professional attitude to the job is concerned. They both want to get an accurate, interesting angle on a story. He does, though, see a contrast in the regional programmes from BBC and ITV. He gave a typical example: 'ITV was showing an item on what women carry in their handbags, with a reporter stopping people in the street and asking to see the contents, while we at the BBC were covering a story on pit closures. There's no saying one approach is better than the other, it just gives the viewer a choice.'

There are regional variations but if, for instance, you are an industrialist, it would be as well to bear in mind that the BBC is likely to look more seriously into your story than some ITV magazine equivalents, where the emphasis may be more on entertainment. So the same story could be treated very differently by journalists working on different programmes. You have everything to gain by making your name with your local media. There are now specialist TV and radio reporters in areas such as:

- education
- environment
- local government
- regional affairs (policing, etc.)
- community affairs
- health
- sport

There are also district specialists dotted about the regions, so it behoves anyone who is interested in promoting a product or service to get to know the journalists.

Roy Saatchi is Head of Local Programmes at BBC North in Manchester, and he feels that industry often does not make the most of media opportunities: 'Get to know us! There is really just one BBC. If you do a piece for Radio Merseyside it is quite likely to be picked up by *The World At One* or *Newsnight*. If you have a story that you know may be of interest to other radio programmes like *Science Now* or *The Money Programme*, then tell the reporter who interviews you and he or she is very likely to put it forward to the relevant department.' But to repeat a point I made earlier, it is essential to know the style of a programme before doing so. Nothing annoys and insults a reporter or producer more than being sent material that is of no use to them because it has no place in their programme; especially as anyone who had done the slightest bit of research would know that!

National News Programmes

Newsnight's most feared presenter is Jeremy Paxman. I managed to catch up with him in a taxi in the middle of a busy day. I asked about the relationship between journalists and politicians. He looked at me with that cool gaze and said: 'It's the old maxim, isn't it? A journalist is to a politician what a dog is to a lamp post.' Before an interview, Jeremy writes down the areas he will cover, but not the questions. He tries, however, to think of an opening that looks at a new angle, something that the politician will not expect. In his opinion, good journalists must be curious; they must want to find out.

As *Newsnight* is an influential programme, interviewees have to know their subject, be well-prepared and know what they want to say. The teams of researchers are expert in finding relevant information quickly, even though they will not be sure who is going to be on the programme until well into the day. Jeremy, though, would never try to discomfit a member of the public, and would be 'gentleness itself' when conducting an interview with someone who was obviously nervous; but woe betide any government minister who tries to pass the buck!

Documentaries

The style of documentaries has changed a great deal over the last twenty years. The main reasons for this have been the growth in the number of hours people watch television, the diversity of programmes and the availability of up-to-the minute news and information. As a nation we are now much better informed.

The journalists who work on investigative documentaries are a pretty hardy breed. They are used to being bullied, harassed and threatened, which only makes then keener. Peter Godwin, who now works on *Assignment* and *Panorama*, has seen his share of danger. As a war correspondent for *The Sunday Times* in Africa he has been shot as well as blown up, so there is very little that will stop him getting to the root of a story. *Panorama* has been the BBC's flagship documentary programme since the days when it was hosted by Richard Dimbleby, and Robin Day and Michael Barratt were two of the reporters. Michael remembers when there were up to four items in every programme. 'I would go into the office and someone would say "Mike, there's a plane leaving at one – be on it." The pace was frantic and often we filmed all week, edited Sunday, voiced the piece on Monday and it went out that night.' Today, the tendency is to concentrate on one in-depth report, although the mere mention of the name *Panorama* is enough to make some people's alarm bells ring.

Peter Godwin says there is no need fo anyone to worry unless they have something to hide! 'There are two approaches journalists use if they want to go for somebody. They either appear to be very friendly, gaining your confidence and encouraging you to drop your guard, or they hand you the loaded gun. "We've already spoken to such a body and they have said this about you, so we are offering you a chance to defend yourself. If you don't say anything, you know how it's going to look."' Before taking that gun you need to consider carefully what the damage would be if you do not appear, and what it could be if you do.

The later in the evening, the more likely it is that people have specifically tuned in to watch or listen to that particular programme. The audience for *Newsnight* is smaller than for the *Nine O'clock News*, but the people watching are using probably seventy per cent of their concentration. All this has a bearing on the amount of research you need to do before agreeing to take part. When television companies undertake to 'expose' an individual, organization or industry, they will sometimes go to almost any lengths to do it if it is thought to be in the public interest.

CONCLUSION

Before agreeing to be interviewed for any programme, find out as much as possible about the format, the presenters and the audience at which the programme is aimed.

chapter six

BLONDES, REDHEADS AND THE DOLLY IN THE CORNER – *the studio and its people*

Studios can be intimidating places if you have never been inside them before. The lights are what most people notice first. They hang from the ceiling in vast numbers capable of lighting every inch of the studio floor. As well as the set – acting as a background for the presenter, reporters and interviewees – there are usually three cameras and various microphones. There is also a video wall for down-the-line interviews. Television monitor screens are strategically placed around the studio floor so that the floor manager can check the output, and the presenter can see the video tape (VT) or film as it is transmitted.

Sometimes your interview will be part of a comprehensive item, in which case it may well be preceded by a piece of film or, more likely, video tape. In that case it is important that you watch carefully because it can give you vital clues as to the angle of the questions. But that is the only time you should watch the monitor. Ask the floor manager to move it if it is distracting you, as shifty sideways glances at your own image are lethal to an impressive appearance. At best, the viewer does not know what you are looking at, and may conclude that, for some reason, you are unwilling to look the interviewer in the eye. At worst, people have been known to 'dry' completely as they watched their own performance live!

A typical news magazine programme requires between sixteen and twenty studio technicians. This chapter explains what the various roles are.

THE GALLERY

The gallery is usually situated above the studio so the director has a bird's-eye view if he or she looks through the darkened windows down onto the studio floor. The technicians working in the gallery include the following:

Producer

The producer is responsible for administration and the budget. He or she will work with the journalists to decide the content of the programme and the length of the items in it.

Director

Directors are in charge of the technical side, such as the cameras and sound, and everybody on the studio floor. They make sure the programme gets on the air, or on tape, as the case may be.

Production Assistant (PA)

It is the PA's job to time all the items as they go through, keeping the director informed by counting down the pieces as they run. She will also keep the presenter, floor manager and camera operators appraised as to the length of each report, link and interview, as well as keeping track of the overall length of the programme.

Technical Manager

The technical manager supervises all the equipment in the control gallery. This will include VT and telecine machines to run any film inserts.

Vision Operator

The vision operator is responsible for picture quality, setting up and exposing the cameras. He or she works closely with the lighting supervisor.

Lighting Director or Supervisor

Lighting makes a big difference to how someone looks on television. Hollywood stars often ask for the same lighting director on every film if he or she lights them well. Their role is to choose the positions and strength of the lamps used, and what coloured gels or special effects are needed.

Electrician

The 'sparks' works with the lighting director, physically putting the lamps in position and adjusting them if necessary.

Engineer

There is always a backroom engineer to monitor the sound and vision desks, and to be on hand if anything goes wrong.

Vision Mixer

The vision mixer's job is to cut the shots from camera to camera on the director's command and mix between VT inserts, captions and various visual effects to provide the studio output.

Sound Supervisors

Usually operating from a separate gallery, the sound supervisor's job is to balance the sound. One of them will be responsible for clipping on your microphone, the most usual of which is a tie microphone. The only problem with these is that they are vulnerable to any fiddling, so try to leave your tie alone. A stand microphone should present no problems as long as you avoid kicking it when crossing or moving your legs (direct contact with the microphone stand produces a deafening noise for the viewers). If a programme includes an audience, then the sound supervisors are in contact with the boom operator. If there is a boom then you have no worries, since it hangs above your head out of the way.

Auto Script Operator

The auto script is the monitor from which presenters read the script. When I first joined the BBC the auto script was typed on a roll of paper before being run through the machine. This caused problems when alterations were made to the running order and a story was moved. The roll had to be cut and then glued together, which often gave rise to the paper getting stuck! Now it is typed into the computer system in the newsroom by a journalist, and electronically operated from the gallery. This can be done by a production secretary or an employee of a company supplying the equipment, such as Autocue. Newsreaders always have a copy of the script to hand in case the auto script goes down.

The system operates by having a piece of angled glass in front of the camera lens. As it is clear glass it does not obscure the camera's view of the presenter. A monitor above or below it displays the script upside down. Because of the angle, the reader sees the script the right way up. In effect, he or she is looking at the lens through the script. An everyday example of this principle is the back shelf of your car and the angle of the rear-view window. You may have noticed that, if sunlight shines on a book placed on the rear shelf, you can see its reflection in your driving mirror; and because you are looking at a double reflection, the print on the book will appear the right way round – simple.

THE FLOOR

On the studio floor itself there are several key personnel:

Floor Manager

The floor manager will usually greet you and show you to the 'green room' or in to make-up. (The green room is an old theatrical term for a place where the actors rest, or wait during a performance. Derived from when most plays were performed on the village green, it is still widely used to refer to the room into which contributors are shown when waiting to go into the studio.) The floor manager will introduce you to the presenter if there is time, and will generally try and make you comfortable. If you need a drink of water or have any queries, the floor manager is the person to ask.

The floor manager co-ordinates everything on the studio floor and is in contact with the director through radio talkback. Apart from relaying the director's instructions, it is his or her job to make sure people are in the right place at the right time. When your interview has finished, wait until the floor manager tells you it is safe to move, as you do not want be seen scrambling out of your seat as if the studio is on fire!

Camera Operators

Even if robot cameras are used, there still has to be someone to operate them (although this would be done from the gallery). The camera operator is in touch with the director via talk-back. He has a camera script giving the order of shots, which may range from a wide shot or long shot to a mid shot or close-up. You will not be conscious of any of this, but you should be aware that you can be seen at any angle at any time! In the gallery each camera has its own monitor screen, enabling the director to choose the shot he wants. Do not be alarmed if a camera suddenly moves off to a different location – the operator will just be setting it up for the next item.

Make-up Artist

You will probably see the make-up artist in the make-up room. If you want your hair washed or to be fully made-up it is as well to let the journalist or researcher know, and then you can be sure there will be enough time before the pro-gramme. Otherwise, the make-up artist will use powder to prevent a shine, possibly some lipstick to add definition to the mouth, then tidy your hair on the studio floor. Lighting these days is not as harsh as it used to be, but I am always guided by the make-up artist because they see how people look on the monitors.

The Edit Suite

The editors are not in the studio or the gallery, but tucked away in an edit suite somewhere near the newsroom. The director or journalist will go through the piece they have shot and make notes. Having decided on the angle, they will go through it again, making more detailed notes. This can often be done 'off line' on VHS using an ordinary video recorder, therefore saving time and money by not tying up the editor or the expensive broadcast-quality equipment. When there is a certain shape to the piece they will go into the edit suite. Although it does not appear on transmission, VT has a burnt-in time code at the editing stage. This is like a superimposed stopwatch which provides a benchmark, so that the editor can cut at exactly the point the journalist wants. Speed and accuracy are what is needed for news items, even more than artistic flair. It always amazes me the way they can take out a breath to shorten something, or mix a shot so that you cannot see the join!

When Things Go Wrong

A director of a regional news programme outlined to me the sort of things that can go wrong in studios. Most news items are shot during the day, edited and then transmitted in the evening. There is usually a shortage of VT or film editors and edit suites. Regional programmes will probably only have two or three, and there is always a queue of reporters waiting to edit their pieces. This means that a number of items are not ready when the programme goes on the air.

On this specific evening, the director was told that a particularly late report would be ready and make its slot. When the time came, however, it was not there. Normally she would go on to the next item, but this happened to be sport, which meant the cameras had to be moved to another position and there was no time. Apart from this, the sports correspondent was not even in the studio! Keeping her head, the director told the presenter to stop reading the link into the piece that was not there and go straight to reading the sport. The late report was eventually transmitted at the end of the programme. It is at times like these that everybody has to work together and keep calm so that viewers are unaware of the chaos that can be raging in the gallery!

CONCLUSION

The blondes and redheads mentioned in the title of this chapter are two different types of television lights, and the dolly is what the cameras and boom microphones are mounted on, enabling them to move around silently and without any vibration. I can still remember turning round in surprise on one of my first shoots when an electrician shouted to the camera man, 'Hey mate, how many blondes and how many redheads?' I just could not imagine where they had hidden all those girls in such a small van!

YOUR PLACE OR MINE?

– the location

W here your interview takes place determines several factors:

- time
- dress
- attitude
- duration
- control

THE OPTIONS

For radio and television you could be asked to go the main studio or a 'remote' (satellite) studio. Alternatively, the crew could come to your office, factory or anywhere that is relevant to the story. The press journalist will either interview you at home or somewhere convenient to you – which could be your office or possibly a restaurant or bar. Again, there are advantages and disadvantages to be weighed.

When You Go to Them – Television

We will start with television because that is probably the most daunting area of the media for most people. News studios these days are getting smaller. Camera angles mixed with visuals make the BBC's *Nine O'Clock News* look as though it is put on the air from a huge studio when in fact it is very small, as is the one that transmits *Sky News*. Once you have given in your name at reception, you are usually met by the person who originally contacted you, or by the floor manager. You may go straight to make-up or be shown into 'the green room'. Here you should meet the presenter who will interview you, but as he or she might be already in the studio, you may meet only as you are about to go on the air.

The benefits of going to the studio are several:

- If it is a live programme, then you know when you are going to be on. You will not be kept hanging around because the duration of the programme dictates the length of time you will be at the studios.
- There are lots of people around who know what they are doing and will put you at your ease.
- If the programme is pre-recorded, producers might be more flexible as to the time you come in, but they have to book the studio in advance.
- You will probably be made-up, which is always a good thing because a very shiny or pasty face can make some people look as though they are guilty before they even open their mouths! For women, make-up can take longer, as they may want to do more than just dab a bit of powder on a heated brow.
- The lighting is generally more flattering in the studio.

The disadvantages are:

- You may have to travel quite a distance to the studio. Some programmes have the budget to arrange for you to be picked up, while others will reimburse you for the use of your own car. Some programmes do not even do that! Again, always ask the researcher or reporter what the options are.

- People tend to get more tense in a studio environment, especially if they are left in the green room with other interviewees.
- There is a tendency to let the tongue run away if you are nervous, so I would advise you to say very little and listen a lot! It is surprising what you can learn about your opponents.

The hospitality suite – or 'hostility suite' as it is sometimes known – does not usually have the appetizing array of alcoholic drinks that it used to, so it is easier to resist temptation. Do resist it! Alcohol does not help to calm your nerves; it takes the edge off your senses; and believe me, you will want all your wits about you when you get into the studio. Wait until after the programme – then it is time to celebrate. Don't drink too much tea or coffee either, for the reasons I mentioned earlier (*see page 75*). Nothing is worse than trying to conduct a serious interview with a full bladder!

Pre-recording

For a pre-recorded interview, you would probably go into the studio in the afternoon to record it 'as for live'. This means that the item would be recorded on video and slotted into the programme without any editing. A studio is as quiet as the grave, and the silence after the words 'Fifteen seconds studio ... quiet please' is shattering. The heartbeat you can hear may not be yours! Even when items are pre-recorded, every member of the crew is on tenterhooks because television is a team effort, requiring everybody to work precisely to time. The advantage of pre-recording is that you can always do it again if you want to, providing the director has time.

'Re-takes'

There are several possible causes of a re-take which are quite beyond your control. A trainee director might need to have another go while gaining experience. I have seen other instances where the news editor or producer has disliked a shot and asked for it to be done again, sometimes throwing the interviewee. When you have done a good piece the first time it is not always easy to replicate the performance. Try and clear your mind of everything you have said before, and listen carefully to the questions. The second interview may not run exactly like the first, but it can give you a chance to improve. If you were happy with your first contribution, you can use the answers you used previously – but the essential thing is to listen to the questions and not to anticipate them. The difference between the professional and the amateur is that the professional can make 'take' thirty sound as fresh as 'take' one. That is what you have to aim for, and the way to achieve it is to believe every take is take one!

The Live Programme

Live studio programmes function quite differently these days. It is not unusual for the live element to consist only of the presenters' links because much of the programme has been pre-recorded. This means that the studio environment is quiet and clinical rather than full of the hustle and bustle of a few years ago. Having said that, it is present policy at the BBC to have as many live contributions as possible, and there is nothing like it to get that adrenalin running!

As a contributor, you could well have the rather strange experience of going into a studio when the show is well underway. Often you will be taken on tip-toe to your interview position while the presenter is talking to someone else. There could be a piece of film or video running, in which case cameras will be moving round and people will be resetting lights, while a make-up artist is powdering somebody's nose.

It is crucial to keep your concentration, as a busy studio can be distracting. Focus your attention on the interviewer and listen to the questions while remembering what you want to say.

Remote Television Studios

There are some small studios that 'inject' items into the main stations. If, for example, you are asked to be a contributor to *Breakfast News* and you live outside London, you would go to your nearest BBC studio and do a 'down the line' to the *Breakfast News* studio at BBC Television Centre in Wood Lane.

In all remote interviews, you talk to the interviewer through a television monitor. This can be quite off-putting. The temptation is to look at the screen, but it actually looks more natural to focus on the camera lens. Down the line is virtually the only time you do look into the lens, as in all other interviews you look at your interviewer. Hopefully there will be an engineer on hand to show you where to sit and to provide you with an earpiece if you need one. I have known interviewees, however, who have been left to their own devices once the harassed journalist has shown them into the studio. Pressure of work sometimes means people have to be in two places at once, so if you are unsure of the ropes tell the journalist as soon as you arrive at the studios.

On Location

The use of lightweight outside-broadcast units enables a reporter or contributor to be interviewed live on location. For these interviews, have a mirror and a comb handy, as it is unlikely that a make-up artist will be around to make sure your hair is tidy or that you have not got lipstick all over your teeth!

When You Go to Them – Radio

Radio stations are generally smaller than those used for television. They are situated either in the heart of the city or, increasingly, on nearby industrial estates. BBC Radios 1, 2, 3 and 4 are based in Portland Place in London with departments sited throughout the regions. Nationwide services understandably have more staff, money and resources than their local counterparts. They are able to spend more time researching projects and can afford to employ accomplished, experienced personnel.

You will either be asked to come to the studio, or you will be interviewed 'down the line' from a small remote studio or over the telephone from your office or home.

Remote Radio Studios

The remote studio is one of the least user-friendly ways to broadcast. The BBC have these unmanned booths dotted around the country. The main reason for using them is quality, as they eliminate the problem of crackling phone lines. Do not be put off when you go into a completely dark room and have to fumble around for the light switch, let alone the marked buttons which you press to put you in touch with the studio engineers. Having donned your headphones or 'cans' you will be given instructions as to what to do next. It can be quite unnerving if you have not used the system before, but the engineers are helpful and will put you at your ease. Practise steady breathing while you are waiting; it does wonders for the nerves!

Try and keep your mind on the points you want to make or the message you are there to give, as it is important not to let the technology distract you from listening to the questions.

The Radio Car

The radio car is another way that interviewees can be brought into the programme. These are specially kitted-out vehicles that send signals straight back to the studio. They are of varying sizes and sophistication, from converted taxis to full-scale mobile studios. They allow you to sit with the reporter as he or she carries out the (usually live) interview, and are used mainly to grab interviewees when there is no time to get them to the studio.

When They Come to You – Television

There are several advantages to being interviewed on your own premises. You can more easily dictate the time of the interview and the style, as well as not having to spend hours travelling to the studios. Your office or factory allows you to make the most of a business opportunity by choosing the area where interview will take place. Although you will not be permitted to make a blatant commercial, why not ensure that the background shows the name of your product or organization by displaying the company logo, a poster or some strategically placed brochures? A pharmacist, for example, might want to be interviewed outside his or her premises (weather and noise permitting) to show its name, rather than being filmed inside an anonymous shop.

The Outside Broadcast

The size of an OB (outside broadcast) unit varies depending on the job. A news crew will probably consist of two technicians and a reporter, while a programme crew comprises a producer or director, production assistant and electrician, and possibly 'grips' (who are in charge of all the cables attaching cameras to the mains or generator) and a make-up artist. There will be a mobile control room or 'scanner' unit which will transmit back to the studio.

Whatever the size of the crew, allow yourself plenty of time! The news crews have several stories to cover each day, and if one runs late they get behind schedule. It is prudent to allow more time than the crew estimates the interview will take. If, however, it is a short news item (a knock-off interview), they could be in and out of your office in under an hour, especially if they have a busy day. This means that there will be little time to set or light the shot, and it is up to you to make sure you look all right. If you do not normally wear make-up, it is not a bad idea to keep some cologne wipes or translucent powder handy to stop your face or forehead shining, as well as a brush or comb.

Reverses

As only one camera is generally used for outside broadcasts, it initially concentrates on the interviewee. This means that facial shots of the interviewer actually asking the questions have to be recorded after the interview. These are known as the 'reverses'. The camera and lights have to be resited before the reverses and are filmed, and this can take time. There is no real need for you to be there at this stage, but there are occasions when it is desirable to ensure that the 'reverse' questions are the same ones you answered!

Reverses are not always used once the piece is edited, but can provide a gap or break in which to edit if the item is too long. This is also the reason for the smiles and nods you sometimes see in the middle of a report (the 'noddies'). Due to time constraints, I have sometimes shot the reverses the day after the interview in a completely different location, and you would never have known!

The Set-piece Interview

If the interviewee is very short of time and the item is important, the producer may do a set-piece interview which involves the use of two cameras – one focused on the reporter and one on the interviewee. This saves time shooting the reverses because the piece is shot as for live, and timed as if it were taking place in a studio. This method is, however, expensive for the programme budget as it means using two camera crews.

Choosing the Location

The reporter or camera operator will choose the spot that best suits them, which may not be best for you. So decide on the location before they arrive and show them straight there.

Certain backgrounds are used to help the viewer identify immediately with the story. As soon as we see an airport we can be fairly sure we are in for a report about travel. If we are shown pictures of a cattle market we are probably going to see a piece about farming. If, however, there had been a film of a family driving along in a car, or a sweeping shot of the Dales, it would take longer to set the scene for those reports.

Problems

There are a number of things that cause problems when filming, especially if you are recording a longer piece. Most cameramen – I say men because the majority are – like to have the chance to show their artistry, and lighting is the thing that takes the time. If they are shooting for a documentary or a pre-recorded programme, they will convert your office into a 'set'. This means moving your furniture, replacing pictures or bringing in plants from reception to make everything look as attractive as possible. Once the lights have been set, there is the problem of noise. Telephones, fax machines, people talking in the office next door, car alarms, sirens and rumbling lorries or planes all make it difficult to record a clean piece that will allow the viewers to hear you without outside distractions. This often means stopping and starting several times, but bear with them – it is in your own interest!

A good rule of thumb is that the filming for an outside broadcast is unlikely to take less than two hours. I remember a location where the cameraman got carried away and completely revamped the whole office, bringing in plants from here and sofas from there until the poor interviewee was totally bemused. When we started to put everything back in its place after the interview, the man suddenly shouted 'Stop!' He said he preferred the new look!

Cameras

Having cameras at your location can cause problems, and it is essential to know where the crews are at all times. The organizers of the Grand National at Aintree learned their lesson in 1993, the year the race was abandoned. Some crews found their way into the weighing room and were able to talk to jockeys and officials before the stewards had time to put out a statement. This obviously created a confused picture. Now the camera positions are fixed, and interviews have to take place in designated areas so that the clerk of the course and the committee know exactly where they are at all times.

Cameras are getting smaller and smaller, so it is quite easy to hide one inside a jacket or even up a sleeve, enabling a director to get shots without you knowing. While I would not advise conducting an elaborate search, it is a good idea to find out what equipment the crew is carrying. There is no law to prevent your premises being filmed from a public highway, so although it may be impossible to stop the crew getting pictures of factory emissions or steaming chimneys, you can guard against wanton shooting within your own boundaries.

Microphones

As with radio, television microphones can be almost undetectable. Do not, therefore, say anything that could be mis-construed while you are with the reporter. Most sound recordists use clip-on tie microphones. These are far less obtrusive than a boom or a hand-held 'stick' microphone. You will be asked to 'give a bit for level' so that the micro-phones can be adjusted to pick up your natural speaking voice. A boom will be used where people are moving around and, for speed, a reporter will be given a hand-held microphone.

A sound man recently told me that the director on a par-ticular shoot once asked him to leave a second tape recorder running. This machine continued recording after the official interview was over, enabling the reporter to catch the inter-viewee off his guard. Although this sort of material proba-bly would not be transmitted, it might influence the way a journalist words his or her introduction. Something else to be aware of is that a 'boom' microphone can easily pick up sound from the other side of a room, so be on your guard!

CONCLUSION

Remember these main points:

- The location and atmosphere of an interview can have a marked effect on its impact.
- In television, the old maxim of a picture being worth a thousand words holds good, and on radio, the environment can play an important role.
- In press terms, the location is obviously less important, but even here it is wise for the journalist and interviewee to feel as comfortable as possible.

- You should neither overestimate nor underestimate the scale of hospitality you offer the media. On the one hand, they do not enjoy being starved of even a cup of coffee, while on the other, they are deeply suspicious of being hijacked by lavish entertainment. Moderation in all things is a good guiding principle.

chapter eight

READ ALL ABOUT IT!
– selling your story

The media can influence government and public thinking, and that influence can be good or bad. The safe haven provided for the Kurds after the Gulf War, for instance, came about only after three days of harrowing pictures that changed governments' policy of 'non-interference'. The Dangerous Dogs Act was a knee-jerk reaction by the home secretary after vivid publicity in the press showing children who had been savaged by dogs. So how can you gain the positive publicity that can be so valuable in helping to promote your cause?

THE PRESS RELEASE

A statement sent to the press in order to generate positive publicity is called a press release. It is essential to target press releases as, if a newsroom regularly receives uninteresting information from a particular organization, a document will be thrown straight in the bin as soon as a journalist sees the all-too-familiar letterhead or logo.

A press release has to be well written and well presented. For television and radio do not use more than a single side of A4 paper, and make sure that the nub of the story is written in big, bold headlines. There is no need to give the journalists too much information – they will get in touch with you if they need more. Newspapers and magazines are slightly different in that, if an article is well constructed, informative and to the point, it can often be reproduced in its entirety. When writing for the press, make sure the important information is at the top of the page, and that the first paragraph containing the message is no more than twenty-five words long.

So many PR companies and publicity organizations make the mistake of hurling as much information at the media as they can, in the hope that some of it will stick! There is absolutely no point in sending press releases to papers or programmes unless you know what material they use. John Gurnett is the producer of the *Jimmy Young* programme and, in common with most other radio and television producers, he receives press releases by the dozen every day. Most of these end up in the bin. He feels strongly that indiscriminate contact gives the PR industry a bad name, and believes much of it is due to PR companies that are paid by the number of phone calls they make or the number of press releases they issue.

To publicize a book, sending a copy with a press release is a good way to grab the attention of a presenter, especially if it is addressed to him or her personally. Again, make sure that the particular presenter interviews authors on their programme, and that it is the sort of book they usually talk about. For local radio or local press, a universal subject must be aimed at the local community. For instance, a regional CBI office might want to publicize a new government grant. Rather than issuing a press release headed 'DTI grants for small businesses', they would have much more impact with a statement such as 'Birmingham small businesses will get a grant from the government'.

Targeting Your Story

Your press release must put your side of the story across convincingly, but it must also contain information that people will find relevant. Human nature is such that we are interested only in something that affects us – whether it is good or bad. If, for example, you are starting a business that will create 100 new jobs, but you are building your factory in what was green belt, you need to take into account the fears raised in the community about spoiling the countryside. People will not be interested in the history of the company and why you need to build a custom-designed factory rather than take up one of the sites on the existing industrial estate. If, on the other hand, the press release tells them that you are aware of the environmental issues and are ready to discuss them, and mentions the benefits to other local businesses of increased trade in the area, apart from the obvious bonus of employment, you are likely to get more column inches and be seen as good news generally!

Children and animals nearly always sell stories, so bear this is mind when looking for an angle for your press releases. If, for example, a new leisure facility is opening, the way to interest local press and possibly radio would be to concentrate on the fact that children previously had to travel ten miles to a similar place, so the new facility will be safer and more convenient, and families on low incomes will save money on bus fares.

DO NOT BANK ON TELEVISION

As with the press and radio, human interest is what sells stories on television, but to get television interested in your story takes quite a bit of thought and no small amount of ingenuity. Television coverage is the icing on the cake

because you can never guarantee that a big news story will
not break and that your item will be dropped as a result.

Apart from interviews, stories for television must be
visual. What might be a very good story for a newspaper
might not be visual enough for television. A piece of land
under threat from motorway construction is more likely to
attract the television cameras on a warm summer's day
when the leaves are green and the flowers are in bloom,
than when it is dull and muddy in the middle of winter. Try
and make the item as action-packed as possible, but be
aware that even the best laid plans can go astray.

Some years ago, the Central Office of Information was
publicizing potential problems on construction sites. It persuaded the BBC to cover the story, and was all set for the
camera crew to come and film the hazards that had been
rigged up on a site in Oldham. The BBC was contacted again
on the morning of the interview, and confirmed that the
crew was coming. An hour later, the COI got a call to say
that a major story had broken and all available cameras
were out on that. So do not be too disappointed if the cameras fail to turn up, and do not spend too much on trying to
attract them.

POSITIVE AND NEGATIVE PR

Avoiding the Negative

Chris Rush is the Public Relations Officer for Salford City
Council. He runs media-awareness training sessions so that
each department has a good idea how the media works and
what it might be looking for in terms of stories.

As Public Relations Officer, I am only as good as the
organization behind me, so I spend quite a lot of time

making the organization aware of the needs of the media.

I never put myself forward for radio or television interviews, but I will allow my name to be used as a local-authority spokesperson, particularly if it's a negative or difficult story. It's much better than an anonymous 'council spokesman'. Salford, like many local authorities, will usually have different spokespeople, depending on the subject. If it is a story about a new road bridge, then the spokesperson should be the paid officer who is in charge of the design. If there is an interview on council policy issues, then a council member would be more appropriate. Whoever it is, the interviewee should be knowledgeable on the subject and be able to talk about it with enthusiasm.

No one should try to manipulate the media, but it is possible to influence it. The government uses 'news management' to schedule the release of news, but lesser organizations can come unstuck. The concept of news management is like a red rag to a bull to some journalists! The best policy is to be as open and honest as possible, but to be aware of how you can influence the way you are regarded by the media.

There is a fine line between getting to know a reporter and trying to buy his or her services. Chris Rush and his team will meet an editor for lunch, or have a drink after work. They also organize football matches with local reporters. This is not done to focus on a particular issue at that time, just to get to know them better, learn how they think and find out what they are looking for. It would be mixture of social chat and talk about the local authority in general terms. He would not use that time to try and get a particular story covered. That might backfire!

Once a negative story breaks there is a damage-limitation

job to be done. If, for instance, a local councillor has put his hand in the till and run off with the money, the story will be printed, no matter how well you know the reporters. If you have been straight with them in the past, however, they will listen more sympathetically. There can still be a plus in otherwise negative publicity. In this instance you could put forward the positive side of the story by saying that it was the council's procedures that picked up the misdemeanour so quickly. Concentrate the action on one individual, not the local authority or company as a whole. Give the journalists as much information as they ask for – if you try and restrict it they will dig for more anyway.

If you are faced with a public-relations disaster, make sure a spokesperson is available immediately. Even if it is your fault, you can inject a positive note by saying: 'As a result of this experience, we are now going to review our policies, and take steps to ensure it can never happen again.' It is important to give the impression that you are happy to talk to reporters when they initially phone you, since you want to encourage them to come to you first, rather than go to other sources for their information. And if journalists get material from other sources, the story is likely to run for a few weeks rather than a few days.

Fairly recently, there was a case of child abuse that was not picked up by the local authority when the social services should perhaps have been more alert. The council's PR department formed a strategy. They did not release any information, but they assumed there would be a leak and had prepared a statement. As soon as the first reporter rang, they put out an announcement to all the press. When the story broke it was on the grounds that a child sex-abuse ring had been smashed. The social services felt so confident, in fact, that they released a story of a scheme to help sex offenders, which got good local coverage.

Another local authority decided to handle a similar situation in a totally different way. The council tried to prevent the press covering the story, and took out an injunction. This was so draconian that it even prevented their own councillors from discussing the issue in the council chamber, which naturally caused some dissent within the council itself. The *Mail On Sunday* decided to fight the injunction and eventually got it lifted. There were front-page headlines saying 'SILENCED!' 'SATAN COUNCIL CONDEMNED' and 'STOP THE BLUNDERS!' There were a great many articles, all with these kinds of headlines, leaving the PR officer an unenviable task in his dealings with the media. It is important to remember that such 'cuts' (newspaper cuttings) remain in the newspaper libraries for ever.

Pushing the Positive

Geoff Simpson is Public Affairs Manager for the Co-operative Wholesale Society. He believes it is important to keep in touch with the media and that it is a two-way process. Journalists are always going to report on the activities of a large organization, so a company should try and have some ability to influence what they say. The better your relations, the more able you are to generate ideas that might appeal to them and might get you some constructive publicity. 'You have to offer the media what it wants, you have to operate on it's terms,' Simpson believes.

The CWS set up a seven-days-a-week, twenty-four-hours-a-day PR service. The PR team's home phone numbers are widely circulated and the security staff are briefed to pass on calls any time of the day or night. They are sometimes set tests, when Geoff Simpson will phone up, even on Christmas Day, pretending to be a journalist. The team persuaded top management that they should also be prepared to help answer questions any time of the day or night. 'If we are got out of bed at two o'clock in the morning, then so are senior line managers. We have earned the reputation of always answering questions honestly, factually and within deadlines. We never say "No Comment".' Once you have earned a reputation for co-operating with journalists, they are more likely to co-operate with you.

The CWS has a relatively small PR department for a company with a turnover of 3.3 billion pounds – seven people based in Manchester. Over the past few years they have developed a system where the large retail operations have a PR manager on their staff with a direct line to Geoff. 'It is impossible to run PR for a large retailer in, say, Glasgow from a base in Manchester. It's such a fast-moving business.'

They also use outside agencies on an *ad hoc* basis, but everything goes through the main PR department. This is essential in any good PR policy, as it is vital that the right hand knows what the left hand is doing. Co-op Travelcare is one of the largest travel agencies in Britain. All the branch managers are given PR training so that each can act as their branch's own PR officer on positive issues. As soon as there is a problem, however, such as a customer complaining about a hotel, the complaint is referred directly to Manchester.

The best PR departments are managed by ex-journalists. A core of people are needed who not only write like journalists, but think like them. The people who work in a PR office must know the difference between a *Guardian* and a *Telegraph* angle, a *Mirror* and a *Sun* angle. They have to be able to spot a picture opportunity and know whether radio or television might be interested in the story, as well as to write press releases that will be published unedited.

Christopher Fildes, the financial columnist with *The Spectator* and *The Daily Telegraph*, gives this advice for dealing with the press:

If a journalist rings the number on the press release and gets the response – 'I'm sorry he's away today, and I don't know anything about it. Could you call back on Tuesday?' – he or she will curse you briefly and move on to the next business. Every day, press offices with hospitality cupboards and designer stationery fall at this first hurdle.

A central PR department can help by writing a generic press release for all their branches, leaving a space for the branch name and the name of the town to be filled in. This can then be sent to the local press and radio stations. Avoid sending long press releases by fax. If the line is blocked by a lengthy incoming press release just as the harassed journalist is trying to send an important piece of news to Washington, it will not endear the sender!

George Westropp, National director of Communications at the accountants Touche Ross, has helped raise the company's profile dramatically over the past fifteen years as the firm has grown into one of the biggest in the country: 'Press coverage can be a powerful tool in selling a firm, just as bad PR can be its downfall – ask Gerald Ratner! Building and enhancing a reputation is rarely straightforward and takes time, effort, careful thought and planning.'

Apart from promoting his own company, Westropp handles marketing for outside organizations. One of his most challenging assignments has been to promote salmon fishing on the River Beauly in Scotland. How do you get the media interested in a rather elitist sport? 'The angle I used was to promote the Beauly as having joined the 'Big Five' salmon rivers in Scotland. There is also a good conservation story, as there are more salmon in the river now than for over 100 years.' Apart from inviting journalists to participate, the outlets for promoting something like this might be in-flight videos and magazines on planes, boats and trains as well as articles in papers such as The *Financial Times* and *The Daily Telegraph*.

Is Any Publicity Good Publicity?

If you have no care for your reputation, then I suppose there is no such thing as bad publicity – indeed, some people will do almost anything to stay in the limelight. It should nevertheless be remembered that 'the cuts' live for a long time, and are not just yesterday's fish-and-chip wrappings. If we use the actress Gillian Taylforth as an example, she may be remembered far longer for her part in the case involving a Range Rover than she will for her part in *EastEnders*. If you take on the press, you have to remember that they hold the trump cards as far as how and when they release the stories they are going to print. Some might say that the best thing Gillian could have done was to live with a small amount of adverse publicity that would soon be forgotten, rather than take a newspaper to court and be splashed all over the front pages of every tabloid in the land.

Some people have made huge amounts of money from publicity that has lifted them from relative obscurity. Take the case of the ice-skaters Tonia Harding and Nancy Kerrigan before the Winter Olympics at Lillihammer in 1994. Whether Tonia Harding was guilty of engineering an attack on her rival proved irrelevant as far as the media was concerned. Both girls sold their stories for huge amounts of money.

Every Picture Tells a Story

What happens when the media creates an image to sell to the public? A satirical programme such as *Spitting Image*, as well as cartoons in the press, can have a big influence on how we see political leaders. In the case of 'the two Davids' (Steele and Owen), *Spitting Image* gave the impression that David Owen dominated the relationship between the two men, and was kicking Steele around. This in itself need not have caused a problem, but it clearly had an effect on Steele. Wherever he went in Britain, addressing meetings as leader of the Liberal Party, somebody in the audience would ask him about the programme.

What can you do to defend yourself? It is obviously very difficult to combat this sort of situation. One option is to ignore it completely. Another is to draw the line of fire away from the cartoon image by showing the press a side of you that has not been seen before and getting them to focus on it. This could be the fact that you are a closet saxophone player, like Bill Clinton, or that you abseil to raise money for charity. Those examples are slightly facetious, but sometimes the bizarre can divert media attention. Most journalists get their information from the cuttings libraries, and if they find something that fires their imagination, it will be used again and again, whether it is true or not!

Pictures can also help to sell or enhance a story. If you want to send to your local paper a picture of a football team receiving a trophy, make sure that the appearance and style of the picture matches that of the paper. Put together with your press release, it is more likely to be printed. A photograph of a new day centre for the elderly is unlikely to make the national media, whereas a picture of a new-born gorilla will! If the paper cannot send a journalist or photographer, then ask them if they would like a photo sent in. Find out what size picture is best and how it should be set out, as there is no use sending in a few distant figures if they want good, strong close-ups. Ensure there is something that mentions the name of your organization in the photo. Write a short piece outlining the importance of the event and the aims of the company, charity or group, as well as the names of all the people in the picture. If they print the photograph and nothing else, you will have gained something!

CONCLUSION

The three main points to remember when selling your story are:

- Make contact with your regional journalists and find out what sort of stories they are looking for.
- Make sure you or your spokespeople are properly prepared.
- Think carefully about the content of your press releases and where you should send them.
- Remember that it is unwise to try and 'buy' a journalist. I heard of one man who spent an evening wining and dining one particular editor who promised to do a large colour spread. Unfortunately, it must have been the wine talking, as he has never heard another thing!

chapter nine

LEARNING FROM OTHERS

One of the best ways to learn is from the experiences of others. How far is it safe to go to accommodate the media and what are the pitfalls? ICI is one company that has had many brushes with the media in the past. Edward Brady is Public Affairs Manager for ICI Chemicals & Polymers in Runcorn, Cheshire. He never has to contact the media if there is a problem at a plant because he knows that the journalists will be there almost before he is! He finds it difficult, however, to attract radio or television interest if he is trying to be proactive with what he regards as a good news story.

He recalls the opening of a new twelve-million-pound plant built to drastically reduce the amount of pollution going into the local waterways. Initially he was delighted with the media response to the opening, particularly by the appearance of a television crew. Delight turned to dismay, however, when he saw the report that evening. The journalist began the piece with an interview from a senior ICI manager, but then intercut it with unrelated footage of a Greenpeace invasion of an adjoining ICI plant twelve months earlier. The report ended with a Greepeace comment on the new plant: 'Too little, too late'. ICI felt aggrieved.

Brady believes that the journalist's drive for balance can give a biased view in some situations: 'At one time we would always appear on television, regardless of the programme. Now we are much more circumspect.' ICI's policy today is to invite the journalist and the producer to come in and talk about the programme, the subject matter and the areas to be covered. They will ask for something in writing to confirm the conversation and lay out the guidelines. Occasionally they may decline to take part, and issue a statement instead. And legal action is not ruled out should a television documentary distort the true picture. 'Although we've had some good treatment from radio, I'm still very wary of TV. We always try to co-operate, but in some circumstances it is clear they are looking for an Aunt Sally. In certain instances we have taken the view that we shouldn't even dignify a particular programme by appearing on it.'

But it is so hard to say no! When ICI were asked by Granada Television to appear live on their early evening programme to answer accusations from villagers in a dispute about heavy lorry traffic, they decided to issue a statement rather than send a spokesperson. They felt that although a heated debate might provide lively television, it would do little to progress the company's case. After receiving the prepared ICI statement, the producer said: 'We'll leave the door open in case you change your mind and want to come down and take part.' Even after being given a firm 'No', and a reiteration that the statement was ICI's only response, the producer repeated his offer. When the programme came on the air, the 'on site' reporter interviewing the villagers turned to the camera and said: 'Well, ICI, we're still waiting for you if you wish to come down and discuss the issue.'

Towards the end of the programme the reporter read out the statement and then repeated the invitation, which naturally left a big question in the viewers' minds as to why a spokesperson for ICI would not come down in person to answer the case – what had they got to hide? Would it have been better to run the risk of a shouting match between thirty angry villagers and one spokesperson from ICI? The company immediately rang the producer and put in a strong complaint. That incident provides a dilemma. What would you do if you have been treated like that? There are two steps that might help:

1) The company could have offered a spokesperson to be interviewed either at the plant or in the studio, on the grounds that thirty to one is not a fair ratio or that a confrontation would only inflame a delicate situation.
2) ICI could have suggested a one-to-one interview with one spokesperson from the village on neutral ground so that a balanced and less emotive argument would result.

If the television company refused the request, the only thing left would be to demand the right to reply. An 'apology' or subsequent interview can be a problem because you cannot be sure that you will be addressing the same audience, but it is far better than nothing and can do a great deal to redress the balance. Edward Brady's advice when confronted with this situation is:

• Talk to producers and reporters before agreeing to take part.
• Find out what they want and get them to confirm it in writing.
• Contact the producer or reporter if you are not happy with the broadcast interview.

THE POLITICIANS

Publicity is part of life if you are in politics. Most politicians need journalists as much as journalists need them. Charles Kennedy, the Liberal Democrat MP, thinks it is vital to foster good relations with the media. Having worked for the BBC in Scotland for a short time, his journalistic training has helped him a great deal, as he knows how journalists think.

Entering Parliament at the age of twenty-three, he was not dealing with senior correspondents but with reporters his own age. They have now grown up together and have formed good relationships, so that if he has something to say, they will listen. He says journalists are always surprised by how much attention MPs pay to what is written about them. His advice is never to believe your own reviews when they are good, but do take notice when they are bad, because more often than not there is a grain of truth in them. Above all, do not take them too much to heart. Any profile is bound to have some criticism in it, but if you feel this is unfair, or factually incorrect, contact the journalist who has written the piece and ask him or her to set the record straight.

Neil Kinnock describes radio, television and the press as 'three countries'. He likes radio country best, as in his view it has a directness and an intimacy about it. Television country is stimulating and creative, but he finds the press country pretty hostile terrain: 'Even when you are accurately quoted, an entirely different impression can by given by the British press's habit of editorializing around the word.' He gave me an example of one occasion when the press chose to quote him. Instead of a straightforward printing of his words, they chose to preface them with 'In a surprising answer, Mr Kinnock said ...'. This is something impossible to guard against. As someone who now presents television and radio programmes as well as contributing to them, Neil

Kinnock's advice is to be as natural as you can. He believes that if you can look relaxed when a load of dinosaurs are cavorting around in your stomach, then you have achieved some kind of broadcasting art!

Sir Bernard Ingham has been press secretary to Dame Barbara Castle, Tony Benn and Lord Carrington, but is probably best known for his time serving Margaret Thatcher. Having worked from seven in the morning until eight at night for over eleven years dissecting the media, writing speeches, arranging press conferences and constantly meeting journalists, he has now gone back to his first love, journalism. His advice to aspiring politicians is have something to say, say it crisply, but do not get over-exposed. He sees no value in becoming a 'rentaquote'. As with anybody in a position of authority, whatever you say must have credibility. If it is controversial, then so much the better, in Sir Bernard's view. He feels many industrialists could take a leaf out of the politician's book when it comes to communicating, and thinks they should make much more of the media.

CHOOSING THE MEDIUM

One of the differences between politicians and industrialists is that the politicians know that as a condition of their existence they have to defend themselves before the nation, whereas industrialists can often get someone else to do it. A member of a large company can nominate a spokesperson, and therefore decide to do only certain interviews, choosing the medium they prefer.

Sometimes you cannot choose the medium – you may be the only person equipped to do the interview so you have to make the most of it. But what if you can choose? You have to look at the tools of your trade. If you have a very good voice, but hate the camera, then maybe radio is better for you. If you are photogenic, but do not sound particularly interesting, then television might suit you better. That is a generalization, but it does provide a starting point.

Some organizations have a policy of choosing a particular person for a particular programme. Again it comes back to the message and the audience. A large utility company, for example, may train several spokespeople to tackle different problems and different programmes. If they are asked to talk about 'electricity' on a children's programme, they might not choose the person who is the most knowledgeable. Somebody with an academic interest in the subject might not be able to put it across in the simple terms that children would understand, but that same person might be ideally suited to explaining it to a trade or scientific magazine.

Equally, if that company offered a representative for a radio phone-in, they might not use the same person for a regional television programme. Why? Well, some people are more at ease in front of cameras than others, some are more photogenic than others and some have a natural wit that shines through in the less intimidating environment of a radio studio. There are also those who have dealt with the press all their working lives, but find it almost impossible to handle a broadcast interview that lasts only two or three minutes. If you are lucky enough to have a number of good communicators at your fingertips, you are able to provide horses for courses.

SPOTTING THE CLOUD

It is important to learn to look at a story from every angle. What may seem at first glance to be a good news story can have a cloud attached to its silver lining. Take as an example a councillor who was asked by his local radio station to come in and talk about a scheme that had been launched to provide free loft insulation for pensioners and one-parent families. He thought he would have the sympathy of the presenter and was rather shocked when the opening question was: 'Don't you think it is irresponsible for the council to be launching this scheme at this time, when the council tax has gone up dramatically and most people are having trouble paying it already?' You cannot assume the journalist or producer will see your story in the same light as you do, and if it makes a better interview to tackle the negative side of the issue, sometimes they will do so. It all comes back to preparation – look at the story from every angle.

THE TECHNOLOGY

Sir Bob Scott, as Chairman of the Olympic Bid Committee, has had many tough interviews to face, but it is not always the journalists who cause the problems – technology can also play its part. The BBC had booked him to appear on the *Nine O'Clock News* on the evening the winning Olympic bid was announced. He was told the piece would be transmitted live at five minutes past nine via satellite from a balcony in Monte Carlo. Sir Bob was waiting with the BBC correspondent and the rest of the crew as the minutes ticked by. 'I was standing there like a lemon for quarter of an hour. I was disappointed, exhausted and people were panting to get me on other programmes. Then suddenly you're on, but nobody watching has any idea that you've just spent fifteen tense and tiring minutes waiting. You just have to take a deep breath and get on with it.'

In his view, the way to cope with that situation is to put yourself into the minds of the producer and interviewer. Their priority is to get you into that programme, and they will do their utmost to do that. Your job is to remain as calm and as alert as you can.

THE HOT SEAT

One man who found the seat quite hot was a senior member of the CWS (Co-operative Wholesale Society) when he was asked to appear on *Kilroy*. The subject was solvent abuse and the problems of children being able to buy solvents over the counter. After the interview, in which he assured the viewers that the policy of all Co-op stores was to prohibit the sale of solvents to children under eighteen, Kilroy showed a film of the producer's ten-year-old son going into several stores – including the Co-op – and buying all sorts of solvents with no trouble at all. Luckily, the CWS's very experienced PR department had taken their man through all the possibilities. He immediately asked to know the name of the store in question, so that after the programme he would get in touch with them to make sure it did not happen again. He also admitted to the difficulties of monitoring that kind of problem and thanked Kilroy for having drawn it to his attention. He was sincere in what he said and gained the audience's respect.

THE INEXPERIENCED JOURNALIST

Before an interview you are unlikely to know what experience a journalist has, but it is as well to find out – tactfully! There are certain questions that can help you build up a picture of the reporter's background, such as 'How long have you been with the BBC?' or 'Have you worked on this paper for long?' and 'Where were you before you joined Carlton?' Luckily, television producers have stopped dragging people off the street to present their programmes in favour of those who have had at least some training, but if the journalist is on his or her first job, it can cause problems for you. A very young presenter conducting her first interview asked me: 'If I ask you the wrong question, will you answer the right one?'

Take the case of a chartered surveyor who was interviewed for a local television evening news programme. The interview seemed to go well and he was pleased with his performance. As he watched the television that night (having rung his family and friends, not to mention some of his clients) he was appalled to see that the only part of him that was really visible was the top of his head. When he went into the office the next day, the first thing people said was 'I didn't know you were going bald!' The reporter was very inexperienced and had not checked the shot with the cameraman. This was during a period in some regions when young journalists who were completely new to television had to be taught by camera crews about how to set up shots and present the news item they were reporting. After a while, the crews naturally got fed up with this addition to their workload, and let the poor journalists (and interviewees) flounder until proper training was introduced.

WHAT TO EXPECT

Sometimes you are not always treated by the media with the courtesy and respect that you might anticipate. Nancy Evans is director of the charity Re-solve which helps fight solvent abuse. She is well aware of how important the right kind of exposure can be, so she will do what she can to accommodate the media. She has, however, had some disappointing experiences. More than once she has spent long hours discussing programmes and then filming, only to find that the item has been dropped altogether or drastically cut: 'They expect you to drop everything at a moment's notice, but they don't realize the inconvenience and cost for a small organisation like ours.' Re-solve now has a full-time information officer to develop media relations in the hope that these instances can be avoided.

But can they? David Shepherd is courted by the media both for his work as an artist and as the founder of his Conservation Foundation and The Somerset Railway. He has had similar experiences, and warns anyone prepared to devote much time to the media, especially television, not to build up their hopes. During one of his campaigns to save the tiger, he was asked by BBC Pebble Mill in Birmingham to set up an exhibition of his paintings in the studio. It was going to be a substantial slot and took much of the day to arrange. Just before he went on the air, the researcher taking him into the studio said 'Awfully sorry, but we've only got three minutes as we've included some other items.' David is a media man and loves the excitement of television, but he was irritated by the cost in time and effort that achieved so little. He is careful now to find out exactly what is involved before committing himself too fully. Most of his experiences with the media have been more positive, however. Magazine articles and radio interviews have given good publicity for the Foundation as well as being pleasant encounters. His advice is to do what you can to help, but realize that, although people often promise the earth, they seldom deliver it.

CONCLUSION

Keep these two main points in mind:

1) Be prepared for the unexpected, both technically and as far as the behaviour of the journalist or presenter is concerned.
2) Try to co-operate, but do not let it cost too much in time or money.

chapter ten

AND FINALLY . . .

Finally, here is a précis and checklist of the main points to remember when dealing with the media. Good Luck!

THE PRESS

- If a reporter approaches you unexpectedly, do not blurt out the first thing that comes into your head. Offer to make some enquiries and call the reporter back. In that time consult someone, or decide for yourself what needs to be said.
- Check the journalist's credentials.
- Keep the interview short and only make statements you have prepared.
- Listen carefully to the questions, and the question behind the question.
- If you are expecting to be in the papers, perhaps because your organization is under attack, try to anticipate what you are likely to be asked – and mentally prepare your response.
- Remember that the newspaper reporter, unlike those of radio and television, will probably interrogate you without prior warning. Questioning which appears to be both friendly and innocuous may be leading you

into a trap.

- If the story is really hot, journalists will surround your workplace round the clock, or ring you up at home at three in the morning!

- As far as newspapers are concerned, female reporters are often twice as smart and ruthless as the men.

- During the face-to-face interview, reporters may use the notebook ploy, asking questions without appearing to take down the answers. Be careful. The notebook may have gone but the interview continues. Remember you are talking 'on the record' the moment the reporter identifies him or herself.

- Very often the journalist already has the story 'in the bag' from other sources, and is approaching you merely for a quote. This means that the story will not disappear because you decide not to assist. You can always ask: 'Have you talked to anyone else about this?'

- 'No comment' can make you sound guilty at worst and evasive at best. Try to say something. There is, on the other hand, one situation in which you must never say anything – when the matter under discussion is the subject of criminal proceedings, termed sub judice.

- The popular papers specialize in what are called 'human interest' stories – stories about people. Remember that no matter how vast, complex and remote your organization may be, it is also involved with people. Do not make the mistake of discounting the importance of one grey-haired little old lady or a tiny tot with golden curls. If they are involved with your organization, one unguarded remark about them can destroy your reputation.

- The press can be used by you – if you say the right

things.

- Generally speaking, the popular papers do not 'make things up'. The problems they cause arise from the tendency to simplify, exaggerate or dramatize the stories they cover. The function of the popular press is to entertain. It is no more sinister than that.
- It is useful to insure yourself against the attentions of the tabloid press by cultivating a relationship of trust with your local weekly or evening papers which are less likely to get it wrong.
- You are unlikely to get a printed apology unless the matter has come before the courts. You are more likely to get satisfaction with a letter to the Editor intended for publication.

TELEVISION AND RADIO

- Do your homework, know your subject.
- Watch, listen and read; get to know the journalist's style.
- Never lose your temper.
- Always listen carefully.
- Learn to read body language.
- If you don't trust the interviewer, think carefully about doing the interview.

Creating a Good Impression on Television

- If you have any visual aids, bring them with you, but not at the last minute. Directors have a lot of things to do with their cameras and your visual aids might well upset their plans, so let them know in advance.
- Sit properly and do not slouch.
- Sit on the tail of your jacket to prevent your collar

riding up.

- Do not wear hound's-tooth-type checks. They make the cameras feel ill. Pastels, blues, creams and pale yellow are safe, and for women, bright colours have more of an impact.
- If you cross your legs, make sure that no distracting stretch of white flesh shows between your sock and the bottom of your trouser, or that skirts are not too short.
- Make sure you cannot see the television monitor in the studio.
- Do not look directly into the cameras – your eyes should be directed towards the interviewer.
- Avoid using notes unless they are essential, then use them openly and not furtively.
- Do not under any circumstances arrive at an interview with a speech which is written out or previously learnt!
- Finally, relax! Do not grip the arm of your chair until the knuckles whiten. Take a series of deep, calming breaths, and remember that it is the interviewer's job to keep things going, not yours.

The Informative Interview

- Two or three minutes is the usual time for this type of interview.
- These interviews are usually painless unless nervousness reduces you to a state in which you appear not to know very much about the subject you are there to discuss. Careful preparation is the key.
- Clarity is essential, so you must be certain about your material.
- Decide which main point you want to put over and make it first, repeating it during the interview. Even a

final re-statement is helpful if the message is important enough, but only in a few words because ending comments can often be cut in mid-sentence, which risks making you look and sound ridiculous.

- Make subordinate points in descending order. This means that if the interview is cut short for whatever reason, only the less important points will go by default.

- The whole point of this type of interview is to elicit information, so the interviewer should have little objection to discussing the question areas with you in advance.

- Do not expect too much in terms of air-time. Although your particular topic is of paramount importance to you, and hopefully to a wider audience as well, it has to fit into a busy programme schedule.

- Think about your audience. Tell them what they need to hear, rather than what you might most enjoy telling them.

The Critical Interview

(see pages 44–46)

- It is quite likely that your interviewer knew nothing about your subject yesterday, and is unlikely to know much about it tomorrow, but today he or she is as big an expert as you are.

- The research team will have dug up the key facts and the presenter will have a very clear line of questioning.

- You will not be told the questions in advance, but you should be given the areas of discussion. Always bear in mind, however, that some interviewers have spent weeks researching your interview, so beware of any skeletons in your cupboard!

- Make clear in advance any areas that you will not discuss. If, despite everything, you are asked such a question, say straight out that it is an area on which you are not qualified to speak.
- Try not to fall for 'the interviewer's nerve' ploy (*see page 45*), and do not try the politician's game of not really answering the question.
- The requirements of this interview are similar to those of any reasonably tough business negotiation. The skill is to be able to remember and apply them in the totally different world of the studio – a world in which your interviewer is completely at home. He or she therefore starts with an in-built advantage over you. But do not forget that you are the expert in your own subject.

Questions to Ask the Journalist

- What is the programme?
- How long will the broadcast interview be?
- Where will the interview take place?
- Where, in the programme running order, will the interview be?
- Who else is being interviewed on the same subject?
- Is it recorded or live?
- Who is the audience?
- What is the first question?

THE PRESS RELEASE

The purpose of a press release is to get journalists to write about you. If you do not want publicity, do not issue a press release. Here are some of the guidelines given by Touche Ross in their PR Manual:

- KISS – keep it short and simple.
- Put the angle that is important to the reader in the first paragraph and put the details at the end.
- If you are aiming at a local paper or trade magazine, spell out the relevant angles in the first paragraph.
- Make sure you give the answers to: Who, What, When, Why, Where and How Much.
- Does it pass the 'so what?' test.
- Make sure the journalists can contact you. Give weekend phone numbers.

The Hook

To catch your fish you need a good hook, such as:

- A list – 'everything you need to know about ...'.
- An anniversary – 'It is now a year since ...'.
- A comparison – 'The difference between ...'.
- A time limit – 'The last chance to ...'.

Following Up

- Follow the releases with a phone call to key journalists to make sure they are aware of it.
- When journalists start to respond, return their calls as soon as possible. If you are not there, make sure somebody can deal with queries.
- Have a copy of the release to hand, as well as some

of the answers to anticipated questions.

- Keep the names of contacts up to date. It will not advance your cause if the journalist receives something addressed to his or her predecessor but three.

- The nearer to a deadline a press release arrives, the less likely it is to be used, so find out when deadlines are. Send your release to national papers in the morning and to magazines a few days earlier. Television and radio need more warning as their items take longer to set up.

ANTI-TENSION RELAXATION EXERCISES

These exercises will help release tension and relax both body and mind. They are useful at any time of stress or fatigue, not only when approaching the media!

1) Stand or sit comfortably and roll the head round gently. Repeat three or four times.
2) Raise arms above the head and stretch to the ceiling, then let them drop, swinging arms down and bending the knees, gradually returning to a standing position. Repeat six times.
3) Roll shoulders up to your ears in a circular movement to try to touch the ears. Hold this position, feel the tension and release. Repeat six times.
4) Push or imagine yourself pushing against a wall about a foot away at shoulder height. Gradually release the tension and allow the arms to fall to your side.

BREATH CONTROL

Breathing correctly is essential for an interesting and relaxed voice. When breathing properly for speech, the following things should happen:

1) The ribs swing outwards and upwards to increase the size of the chest.
2) The diaphragm (a dome-shaped muscle) drops and the chest increases in capacity so that more breath fills the lungs.
3) The diaphragm then rises while the ribs are still in the raised position and air is expelled.
4) The ribs drop again and more air is expelled.
5) Sound is caused by the breath striking the vocal cords. Tension makes breathing shallower, affecting the voice.

Practising breathing exercises such as the following will help you develop control over the muscles so that you can use your voice at different levels:

- Stand in as relaxed a position as possible with your head in a comfortable position. Place hands on lower ribs. Breathe in through the nose, and feel the ribs move outwards. Breathe out and feel the ribs swing in. Breathe in to count of three. Hold for three, let out for three. Gradually build up the count. Breathe in while humming and fill the passages in your head. Feel the head throbbing.
- Try reading a poem or a passage of prose and mark the places where you need to breathe. Whisper the piece, then gradually increase the volume. Be aware of the lips, mouth and tongue. Practise saying words in an exaggerated way so that you can feel the

tongue, lips and mouth moving.

EIGHT POINTS FOR CLEAR SPEECH

1) Pace – Vary your speed.
2) Pitch – Not too high or low. Feel comfortable but make sure it varies.
3) Phrasing – Think about what you are saying. Emphasize the main points.
4) Projection – Not shouting. Produce your voice with plenty of controlled breathing.
5) Pause – Very important. It gives your audience a chance to absorb what you are saying.
6) Posture – Relaxed and upright. It is not just for appearance, but essential for correct breathing.
7) Preparation – Essential.
8) Practice – Makes perfect.

VOICE CONTROL

If you are tense when talking, your voice will reflect this. It will be tight and dull and you will not be able to put over your message effectively. Here are a few exercises to help (not to be done in public!). All these exercises work on different levels. They help to open up the voice and make you more relaxed and confident. A calm mind will control the body and nervous system, and a relaxed body can help you achieve a quiet mind!

- Stand in a comfortable position, then drop your head forward.
- Bring your head up slowly and move it from side to side.

- Pull faces and stick out your tongue to ease facial tension.
- Shake your shoulders.
- Shake the wrists.
- Take in some deep breaths, slowly in, slowly out. Repeat three times.
- Tense your whole body, then relax it, feeling the difference.

The following exercises are very helpful if you want to improve the expression and colour of your voice. It is a good idea to record yourself, so that you can hear the difference as you become more familiar with the exercises.

1. Expression

Say aloud: 'It's a good book'.
With more feeling: 'It's a very good book'.
Aim the pitch at the top: 'It's a marvellous book'.
Normal: 'It's a good book.'
Down a bit: 'It's a boring book'.
Right down: 'It's a horrible book'.

2. Control

Take a deep breath before saying each of the following sentences in order to increase breath control. Raise and lower the pitch of your voice with the appropriate words. Be aware of the difference:

I can make my voice climb higher and higher and higher.
I can make my voice go lower and lower and lower.
I
I can
I can control my
I can control my breath
I can control my breath and
I can control my breath and sustain
I can control my breath and sustain my
I can control my breath and sustain my phrasing.

3. Tongue Twisters

These exercises are marvellous for limbering up the tongue, especially early in the morning, or when you are very tired. They are also important because they improve diction and help train the mind and mouth to keep in gear. I always say them on my way to the studio! Start by saying them slowly, pronouncing every letter, then gradually increase the speed.

Betty Botter bought some butter,
But said she my butter's bitter.
If I put it in my batter,
It will make my batter bitter,
So she bought some better butter,
And it made her batter better.

Peter Piper picked a peck of pickled peppers,
If Peter Piper picked a peck of pickled peppers,
Where's the peck of pickled peppers Peter Piper
  picked?

Say these three times:

She sells sea shells on the sea shore.
The Lieth police dismisseth us.
Red leather, yellow leather.
Red lorry, yellow lorry.

I hope these exercises and tips will help in everyday conversation at work or at home, not just when preparing for an interview, as good communication is vital to success in any field.

Good Luck!

chapter eleven

DIRECTORY OF MEDIA OPPORTUNITIES

This section is a guide to the type of programmes to which you are most likely to be asked to contribute, and to the sort of interview you can expect. Programmes change all the time, but the guidelines remain basically the same. It is meant for quick reference. The term 'human interest' is used to cover such areas as health care, hygiene, fitness, children, families, pets, leisure – anything, in fact, that interests us humans!

EARLY MORNING TELEVISION

Business Breakfast (BBC1)

CONTENT
Business reports; interviews with industrialists on topics of national interest. The programme is also broadcast on the World Service, so gaining an international market. Short interviews, either in the studio, or down the line. Recorded features at factories or places of work.

STYLE
Information-seeking interviews, two to three minutes long. They are not out to stitch you up, but need good interesting

topics and people.

AUDIENCE
Business.

TRANSMISSION
Live. Five days a week.

Breakfast News (BBC1)

CONTENT
National and international news items. Interviews with politicians and the general public who are making the news.

STYLE
Short, incisive interviews, running two to three minutes or less.

AUDIENCE
Business people, working mothers, *Guardian* readers!

TRANSMISSION
Live, with both live and recorded features and interviews. Five days a week.

GMTV (ITV)

CONTENT
News and entertainment. Items about and interviews with celebrities, members of the public and politicians. Fitness slot.

STYLE
Longer, informal, chattier interviews concentrating more on the human angle.

AUDIENCE
Housewives, part-time workers, a slightly younger group than the BBC. Across the spectrum audience.

TRANSMISSION
Most interviews are live. Five days a week.

Sunrise (Sky News)

CONTENT
News from around the globe. Longer, more in-depth interviews than *Breakfast News*, but following the same format.

STYLE
Well-researched, informative interviews.

AUDIENCE
Similar to that of BBC *Breakfast News*. News on the hour, every hour.

TRANSMISSION
Live. Five days a week.

The Big Breakfast (Channel 4)

CONTENT
Wacky, zany items aimed at children and the under twenty-fives. Celebrities interviewed on the bed with Paula Yates.

STYLE
Way out!

AUDIENCE
Children, teenagers and those in their early twenties.

TRANSMISSION
Live. Five days a week.

DAYTIME TELEVISION

Kilroy (BBC1)

CONTENT
Studio audience participation on human-interest topics. The audience is recruited from the viewers, and everyone has an axe to grind about the topic of the day.

STYLE
The 'professional' or person in one of the 'hot seats' has to be able to fight his or her corner and answer (often hostile) audience questions. Not too much information volunteered beforehand. Could be in a no-win situation. Think carefully before accepting this one.

AUDIENCE
Housewives, shift-workers, the unemployed, pensioners.

TRANSMISSION
Some shows are live, others are recorded 'as for live'. Five days a week during the series.

The Time, The Place (ITV)

CONTENT
Similar format to *Kilroy.*

STYLE

The presenter does not 'roam' quite as freely with the microphone, and protects the contributors slightly more. Again, think about it.

AUDIENCE

Similar to that of *Kilroy*.

TRANSMISSION

Partly live, partly recorded. Five days a week during the run.

Esther (BBC 2)/Vanessa (ITV)

Afternoon 'chat' shows. Similar format to the two above, but with a softer edge and giving more advice. Guests include experts on the issue of the day and celebrities.

This Morning (ITV)

CONTENT

Set slots: medical, agony aunt, cookery, etc. Takes 'strands' produced by independent companies on topics such as fashion, health and interior design.

STYLE

Very slick and chatty. You will have a good level of contact with the research team beforehand.

AUDIENCE

Housewives, pensioners, part-time and shift-workers, the unemployed, students.

TRANSMISSION

Features are pre-recorded, interviews are live. Five days a week during its season.

Good Morning with Anne and Nick (BBC 1)

CONTENT
Similar to *This Morning*.

STYLE
Slightly 'cosier' than its rival, and the interviews are longer. Again, the researchers will look after you well.

AUDIENCE
Similar to that of *This Morning* but fewer students.

TRANSMISSION
Live. Five days a week during its run.

Pebble Mill (BBC1)

CONTENT
Celebrity-based, and includes at least one music item.

STYLE
Chatty, friendly interviewing style. Presenters have occasionally tried to explore the personal side of guests' lives, rather than the book or play they are there to promote.

AUDIENCE
Housewives, pensioners, shift-workers, the unemployed, schoolchildren home for lunch.

TRANSMISSION
Live. Five days a week during its run.

Living Magazine (UK Living)

CONTENT
Family-based entertainment, as is most of the output on this satellite channel. The programme contains human-interest features, consumer advice and celebrity interviews. Production teams are usually relatively small. Slightly longer than usual interviews of up to five or six minutes in duration.

STYLE
Informal and friendly.

AUDIENCE
Aimed at women and families at home, but gaining a smaller audience than the terrestrial channels.

TRANSMISSION
Recorded. Repeated during the day, five days a week.

Advice Shop (BBC1)

This is typical of several consumer-related programmes on regional and satellite television. They work broadly to the same formula.

CONTENT
Home products and customer-service features.

STYLE
Friendly but informed, seeking the best advice for the viewer.

AUDIENCE
Pensioners, the unemployed, housewives, part-time and shift-workers.

TRANSMISSION
Recorded. Weekly during its season.

NATIONAL NEWS

The news output on BBC, ITV and Sky News is much alike. The interviews are news-reactive, live or pre-recorded, and last on average between one-and-a-half and two-and-a-half minutes. The style is not aggressive or particularly intrusive, but they need informed, succinct interviewees. All channels are in the race to get the story first.

EARLY EVENING TELEVISION

Regional News Programmes and Magazines (BBC1)

CONTENT
The programmes vary only slightly from region to region, with the emphasis more on news.

STYLE
Similar presentation format to the national news, with smartly dressed presenters. Interviews last for around three to four minutes, and depending on the region, will be about industry, employment or welfare. There are very few frivolous items. Sport is also featured quite heavily. The journalists tend to specialize, and usually carry out thorough research.

AUDIENCE
Business people, pensioners, families.

TRANSMISSION
Live, with both live and recorded interviews and features. Five days a week.

Regional News Programmes and Magazines (ITV)

CONTENT
This varies according to the individual television company. Although it is news-based, the emphasis is usually more on entertainment and finding the lighter, more unusual feature.

STYLE
More informal than the BBC on the whole, and can be more controversial.

AUDIENCE
The ITV regional magazines are aimed at a younger audience as well as families, pensioners, the employed and the unemployed.

TRANSMISSION
Live, with both live and recorded interviews and features. Five or six days a week.

Watchdog (BBC1)

CONTENT
Consumer complaints. Like *Kilroy*, it advertises for them.

STYLE
Slightly abrasive; out to catch the villain of the piece; stands up for Mr and Mrs or Ms Average when it comes to goods and services. Has an influence and can make or break a firm's reputation.

AUDIENCE
Families, anyone with a grievance!

TRANSMISSION
Live. Weekly during its run.

The Money Programme (BBC2)

CONTENT
Business-based, providing analysis from the City, business news and interviews with chief executives and directors of companies making the news.

STYLE
Straight and businesslike, seeking information.

AUDIENCE
Industrialists and business people, graduates.

TRANSMISSION
Recorded. Weekly during its run.

Regional television Programmes

BBC regional studios and ITV companies have specific slots for local documentaries that focus on regional issues. The research varies on the size of the production teams, and the programmes are open for tenders from independent companies. They can be quite hard hitting, depending on the subject, so make sure you get a clear idea of the brief, and prepare in advance. They are almost always pre-recorded.

EVENING TELEVISION – DOCUMENTARIES

The more serious documentaries are transmitted later in the evening. They demand a high level of research and experience from production teams, and delve into the depths of an issue, getting to the crux of the problem. They are almost all pre-recorded and the interviews are edited. Documentaries have seasons, or 'runs', but their aim is to look behind the facts as they are presented to the world, in search of the truth as they see it.

World in Action (Granada Television)

CONTENT
Issues from at home and abroad, sometimes requiring undercover research that could take months.

STYLE
Hard hitting and uncompromising. They are out to get the story. Take advice before agreeing to appear if you are defending your reputation, organization, product or service.

AUDIENCE
Students, working people, families, but predominantly over twenty-fives.

TRANSMISSION
Recorded. Weekly during its run.

Panorama (BBC1)

CONTENT
Similar to *World in Action*, but not accountable to advertisers, so there are no 'no-go' areas. Highly experienced

journalists cover national and international events. If you are asked to appear on either of these programmes, make sure you are fully prepared, because they will be!

STYLE
Similar to *World in Action*.

AUDIENCE
Similar to that of its ITV rival.

TRANSMISSION
Recorded. Weekly during its run.

The Brief (Channel 4)

This is one of a series of documentaries commissioned by Channel 4 and made by independent companies.

CONTENT
Legal issues affecting the public.

STYLE
Professional, fairly short items that do not always go into too much depth.

AUDIENCE
Those who are anxious to learn more about the subject. These programmes have small but committed audiences.

TRANSMISSION
Recorded. Weekly during its run.

Secret Service (BBC1)

CONTENT
Undercover spying on public services.

STYLE
Be prepared for the unexpected.

AUDIENCE
A broad spectrum.

TRANSMISSION
Recorded. Weekly during its run.

NEWS PROGRAMMES

Newsnight (BBC1)

CONTENT
Interviews and reports on up-to-the-minute events, often as they happen.

STYLE
Informative and sometimes challenging interviews from well-informed journalists.

AUDIENCE
Working and business people, industrialists, anyone interested in news.

TRANSMISSION
Live with some recorded interviews. Five nights a week.

World News Tonight (Sky News)

CONTENT
News as it happens from around the world.

STYLE
Interviews of three to four minutes or longer in duration.

AUDIENCE
Similar to that of *Newsnight*, but smaller.

TRANSMISSION
Live with some recorded interviews. Nightly.

NATIONAL RADIO PROGRAMMES – NEWS

Today (Radio 4)

CONTENT
News and current affairs.

STYLE
Fast moving; can be quite abrasive. Interviews are in the studios at Portland Place in London, 'down the line' or telephone.

AUDIENCE
Over thirties, drivers, fairly up-market.

TRANSMISSION
Live with some recorded interviews. Six days a week.

The Breakfast Programme (Radio 5 Live)

CONTENT
News and current affairs, sport.

STYLE
Fast moving; short interviews.

AUDIENCE
Under-thirties, business people, sports fanatics, drivers.

TRANSMISSION
Live. Seven mornings a week.

The Magazine/Midday with Mair (Radio 5 Live)

CONTENT
News, current affairs, human interest, music, sport.

STYLE
Fairly fast, with interviews lasting around two-and-a-half minutes. Information gathering.

AUDIENCE
Similar to that of *The Breakfast Programme*.

TRANSMISSION
Live. Five days a week.

The World at One (Radio 4)

CONTENT
News and current affairs.

STYLE
Similar to that of *Today*, but the interviews are slightly longer.

AUDIENCE
Similar to, but smaller than, that of *Today*.

TRANSMISSION
Live but with some interviews pre-recorded in the morning, between 11 a.m. and 12.45 p.m. Five days a week.

Ruscoe on Five/John Inverdale Nationwide (Radio 5 Live)

CONTENT
Ruscoe is aimed more at women, but both programmes have a diversity of topics ranging from dyslexia through electioneering, to cinema, Northern Ireland and sport.

STYLE
Fast, short interviews, studio discussions.

AUDIENCE
Women at home, students, sports lovers, drivers.

TRANSMISSION
Live. Five days a week.

PM (Radio 4)

CONTENT
News and current affairs.

STYLE
Similar to *The World at One*.

AUDIENCE
Similar to that of *Today*.

TRANSMISSION
Live. Five days a week.

The World Tonight (Radio 4)

CONTENT
News and current affairs.

STYLE
Slower pace than *PM*, with more analysis.

AUDIENCE
Drivers, pensioners, people listening in bed.

TRANSMISSION
Live. Five nights a week.

News Talk/Night Extra (Radio 5 Live)

CONTENT
News, current affairs, sport.

STYLE
Interviews on a wide range of topics from home and abroad, looking outside the parameters of Radio 4.

AUDIENCE
Anyone awake!

TRANSMISSION
Live. Nightly.

Midday Edition (Radio 5 Live)

Truncated weekend edition of the weekday programme.

The World This Weekend (Radio 4)

Hour-long edition of the weekday programme.

RADIO MUSIC PROGRAMMES

The Jimmy Young Programme (Radio 2)

CONTENT
News, current affairs, information, music.

STYLE
Informed and friendly.

AUDIENCE
Over forty-fives, pensioners, housewives, drivers.

TRANSMISSION
Live. Weekdays.

Susannah Simons (Classic FM)

CONTENT
Mainly music, current affairs and celebrity interviews.

STYLE
Relaxed, professional and informed.

AUDIENCE
Music lovers, housewives, pensioners, drivers.

TRANSMISSION
Live. Five days a week.

The Gloria Hunniford Programme (Radio 2)

CONTENT
Guests are usually celebrities or 'names' who are promoting books, films, records or plays. Gloria Hunniford has a large audience, and a production mentioned on her show will drive box-office profits up by thousands of pounds.

STYLE
Easy-going, relaxed and chatty, she will make you feel very much at home.

AUDIENCE
Over-forties, housewives, pensioners, people at work, drivers.

TRANSMISSION
Live. Five days a week.

The John Dunn Programme (Radio 2)

CONTENT
Music, celebrity interviews, unusual human-interest interviews.

STYLE
Very relaxed and well prepared; will put even the most nervous interviewee et ease.

AUDIENCE
Drivetime, across the spectrum of the over-forties.

TRANSMISSION
Live. Five days a week.

The Jamesons (Radio 2)

CONTENT
Human-interest stories and interviews.

STYLE
Relaxed and chatty, with a lot of banter between Derek and Ellen.

AUDIENCE
Mainly the older end of the scale; drivers.

TRANSMISSION
Live. Five nights a week. An independent production.

Classic Reports (Classic FM)

CONTENT
Music, news and interviews.

STYLE
Information-seeking interviews with celebrities and people making the news.

AUDIENCE
Drive-time.

TRANSMISSION
Live. Five evenings a week.

Judy Spiers (Radio 2)

CONTENT
Music and celebrity interviews.

STYLE
Chatty and well-researched.

AUDIENCE
Drivers, families at home, aimed mainly at women.

TRANSMISSION
Live. Every Saturday morning. Another independent production.

RADIO TALK PROGRAMMES

Woman's Hour (Radio 4)

CONTENT
Women's issues.

STYLE
Very professional, with well-crafted interviews.

AUDIENCE
Women of all ages and different backgrounds; men at home or in the car.

TRANSMISSION
Live with live interviews and recorded features. Five mornings a week.

You and Yours (Radio 4)

CONTENT
Consumer issues.

STYLE
Well-researched interviews and features. Have been known to try a gentle set-up. Make sure you get sufficient information, and hear pre-recorded pieces if they are relevant to your interview.

AUDIENCE
Housewives, pensioners, drivers.

TRANSMISSION
Live. Five days a week.

The Food Programme/Money Box Live/Science Now/Medicine Now/Law in Action (Radio 4)

The content of all these programmes is specific to their particular subject. They have experts to talk about certain topics and members of the public when appropriate. The interviews are to find out more about the subject, and they do not usually have a hidden agenda. The style varies, as does the make-up of the audience, and the interviewees need to know their subject and be able to talk about it with enthusiasm. With the exception of *Money Box*, these programmes are pre-recorded, and run weekly for a season.

RADIO DOCUMENTARY PROGRAMMES

File on Four/Analysis (Radio 4)

CONTENT
In-depth look at a topical subject, such as the impact of forthcoming local elections.

STYLE
Analytical, probing. When being interviewed on this sort of documentary programme, there is always a hidden agenda.

AUDIENCE
Reasonably small, but committed.

TRANSMISSION
Recorded. Weekly for a season.

RADIO ARTS PROGRAMMES

Classic FM, Radio 4 and Radio 3 as well as BBC local radio and specialist stations have their own arts programmes. If you are an artist, author, actor, playwright or novelist, you could be asked to contribute to talk about your latest work. However successful that work, you will not be asked back if you cannot talk about it using the three 'E's: you need the *energy* in your voice, *enthusiasm* and knowledge about your subject and, above all, you need to *enjoy* telling us about it!

Kaleidoscope (Radio 4)

CONTENT
Arts magazine. Items on the theatre, books, television, the media, films, art.

STYLE

Informed and well-prepared interviews. Needs interesting and lively interviewees to enhance the products.

AUDIENCE

Informed and slightly 'arty', women at home, pensioners, drivers.

TRANSMISSION

Live. Daily.

RADIO PROGRAMMES FOR ETHNIC MINORITIES

There are programmes on both radio and television that cater purely for ethnic minorities, and they, like other programmes, are keen to hear from people from all walks of life. The programmes and producers' names are listed in the television magazines, so if you have a story you feel they should be aware of, get in touch.

FURTHER READING

Cartwright, Sue and Cooper, Cary. *No Hassle*, Century Books, 1994

Curran, James and Seaton, Jean. *Power Without Responsibility*, University Paperbacks, Methuen and Co. Ltd., 1991

Day, Sir Robin. *The Grand Inquisitor*, Weidenfeld and Nicholson, 1991

Greenslade, Roy. *Maxwell's Fall*, Simon and Schuster, 1992

Lidstone, John. *Face the Press*, Nicholas Brealy Publishing Ltd., 1992

Paxman, Jeremy. *Friends in High Places*, Michael Joseph, 1991

Stapely, Sue. *Media Relations for Lawyers*, The Law Society, 1994

INDEX